TIMEWEAVER

TIMEWEAVER

THE BOOK OF NAINOA

HANK WESSELMAN, PHD

NAINOA KANEOHE

ALSO BY HANK WESSELMAN

www.sharedwisdom.com

The Spiritwalker Books

Spiritwalker: Messages from the Future

Medicinemaker: Mystic Encounters on the Shaman's Path

Visionseeker: Shared Wisdom from the Place of Refuge

(*Timeweaver* is the fourth book in this series)

The Journey to the Sacred:
A Guide to Traveling in the Spiritual Realms

Spirit Medicine:
Healing in the Sacred Realms (with Jill Kuykendall)

The Bowl of Light: Ancestral Wisdom from a Hawaiian Shaman

The Re-Enchantment: A Shamanic Path to a Life of Wonder

VISIT THE WEBSITE:

www.sharedwisdompaintings.com to view:

Cover artwork by Hank Wesselman entitled: *Heiau of the Sun*

And other original artwork by Hank Wesselman, including:

- Visionary paintings gallery

- Landscape paintings gallery

- Art school paintings gallery

Original artwork on cover entitled: *Heiau of the Sun* by Hank Wesselman

Editor: Jill Kramer

Book formatting by: Robert Harrison

Cover design by: Wonderburg at 99designs.com

Published in the USA by: Jill Kuykendall

First printing, 2023

ISBN: 979-8-218-07486-9

eBook ISBN: 979-8-218-07487-6

PREFACE

(This preface was written by Hank prior to his passing in 2021.)

My first book, *Spiritwalker: Messages from the Future*, was published in 1995. It received a wide readership in North America, where it was critically acclaimed and then republished in more than a dozen languages abroad. Over the 25 years since, at countless bookstore talks, conference presentations, and experiential workshops, I've been asked to reflect on the content recorded in that book and the two volumes that followed: *Medicinemaker: Mystic Encounters on the Shaman's Path*, and *Visionseeker: Shared Wisdom from the Place of Refuge*.

This trilogy records an ongoing series of spontaneous visionary experiences that began in 1983 and have continued off and on to this day. I have often referred to them as "unorthodox" or "unusual" because in my professional life, I work in mainstream science as a paleoanthropologist and have a doctoral degree from the University of California at Berkeley. I've been a university and college adjunct professor for more than 40 years; and since 1971, I've also been a primary investigator on several international research expeditions, where I've engaged in fieldwork in the fossil beds of eastern Africa's Great Rift Valley in search of answers to the mystery of human origins.

The Spiritwalker series is not about science, however. The books extend beyond science in much the same way that metaphysics extends beyond physics. Science is superb at investigating and describing the physical world, yet metascience investigates and attempts to experience and describe the subjective human experience behind that which we all accept as "the objective real."

Shamans know from direct experience that there is more to reality than what we can see with our everyday eyes. These spiritual practitioners possess the ability to achieve expanded states of awareness in which they use their own bodies and minds to create a bridge between the physical world of form and the transpersonal worlds of the spirits. Within their communities, shamans are the mediators between the world of things seen and the worlds of things hidden, and many become powerful healers.

In 1986, while living on Hawai'i Island, a most

extraordinary story began to be revealed to me—one in which my conscious awareness traveled beyond my body to merge with the body, mind, and soul of another man who lives in another slice of time. But these were not what some call past-life experiences, and as they deepened, I came to understand that I'd been given a look at the future, or to be more precise, a period roughly 5,000 years after the collapse of Western civilization. To say that I was surprised would be an understatement of vast proportions. I was stunned, and thrown into a psychological crisis that took years to fully accept and understand.

Some might call these episodes serial dreams or dreamlike experiences. Others, including myself, came to label them as "shamanic journeys across the Space-Time continuum between the now-here and the now-there." What I saw and experienced within these episodes was intensely real, and my inner scientist felt compelled to take extensive notes. Eventually, in my life that was dominated by teaching and research as well as my family, several boxes filled with yellow pads became the beginning of the narrative flow recorded in the Spiritwalker series.

I was aware when I began to write that most of my colleagues, allies, and adversaries in my academic circles might exert considerable effort to *not* be aligned with such heretical ideas and experience, and regard such literary endeavors as assured "career-icide." Yet following the publication of these books, I was invited to speak at national and international conferences on science and consciousness. I also started to design and teach experiential workshops at well-known retreat and conference centers across the Americas and abroad, bringing me into connection with many others who have the ability to "vision."

My training workshops have been designed to draw the visionaries and mystics among us into connection with each other, then to collectively engage in experiential exercises enhanced by monotonous percussion (shamanic drumming) to access expanded levels of consciousness, allowing us to travel to specific coordinates in the inner worlds and then compare notes afterward about our discoveries. I've been engaged in this endeavor for more than 30 years, and I've discovered—as have countless mystics before me—that these inner realms are inhabited by transpersonal forces that the traditional people call *spirits*.

I experienced many of these spirits as benevolent, helping beings on the one hand, and as the more remote Higher Organizing Intelligences on the other, some of whom are in service to humanity as spirit teachers and guides. Others are rather neutral with relation to humans, and then there are some that are best avoided. The workshop gatherings also allowed the participants to activate an ongoing connection with what appears to be our personal Higher Selves or immortal Oversouls (a term coined by Ralph Waldo Emerson).

In time, the nature of the spiritual dimensions and my

ongoing connection with these transpersonal forces provided me with an inescapable conclusion: Our minds appear to be part of a matrix of countless minds at large upon planet Earth, only some of which happen to be human. The role of the shaman is, and has always been, to be the inspired visionary who is in a conscious relationship with these other awarenesses. In this regard, allow me to observe that for those who judge this to be wishful thinking or delusional daydreaming, there exists a substantial body of literature, gathered by scientific investigators, to back up every point I have made above . . . so let us proceed.

In the middle 1980s while living on my family's small farm on Hawai'i Island (also known as the Big Island) and teaching at the local branch of the university, my conscious awareness was drawn into connection with the mind and soul of a man who lives in the distant future. He is an individual of Hawaiian ancestry named Nainoa, and with repeated contacts across many years, I came to understand that he may in fact be one of my descendants, perhaps even a descendant self. The connection, when it happens, resembles what some might call spirit possession; yet in this dynamic, my conscious awareness appears to be the possessing visitor, taking up temporary residence in this other individual's body in his slice of time. Periodically, this bizarre connection also began to occur in reverse, with Nainoa taking up temporary residence within me in *my* slice of time here. My thoughts about this strange crisscross phenomenon have been carefully described in the three aforementioned books.

These experiences are intensely real. When I am in connection with Nainoa, it is as if I *am* him, as if I am *there*, and I mean *really* there. And this is where it gets sticky, because in these expanded states of awareness, I seem to be time-traveling, literally; yet as described in my other books, it is an aspect of the soul/mind complex that travels—not the body. These experiences brought out the curiosity of my inner scientist with relation to Time and Dreaming … and what Time may actually be (I am capping these terms with intention).

In retrospect, these visions were much like memories, but memories of the future, if such a thing is possible. Trying to understand the nature of this phenomenon became a kind of obsession for me. It also became a shared area of focus in my friendship with a Hawaiian kahuna elder named Hale Kealohalani Makua over the last eight years of his life. Interestingly, with relation to Time, Makua observed more than once that "the future actually came first, and that we are living in the past," a paradox he did not explain, yet he invited others to discover the significance for themselves.

Timeweaver is the fourth book in my Spiritwalker series. Throughout all these works, there exists a strong overlay of appreciation and respect for many aspects of indigenous spirituality and mysticism, culture, and thought—aspects that are currently being reconsidered in our Western world in response to the fact that an entirely new spiritual complex is currently taking form. It is solar based and interactive and stands on a time-tested mystical foundation that may eventually enrich, supplant, or completely replace all of our current organized religions. Our relationship with Nature seems to be the key that opens that door.

Now let me say a few words about the man named Nainoa who has served as my "informant" for several decades. As I've mentioned, he is originally of Hawaiian ancestry, yet he is not geographically located in Hawai'i. He appears to be living somewhere on the western coast of North America in a region now known as California. I say *living* in the present tense because when I have access to him and the experiencing of his world through him, it is perceived as *now*.

Let me add that when I am merged with him, our respective mental and emotional levels of being become a multidimensional mosaic of experience, with my own thoughts and feelings thrown in next to his.

In the beginning, Nainoa was completely oblivious to the presence of my mind nested within him. Yet as the experiences continued, he slowly became aware of me. And surprisingly, it was his conviction that I must be one of his ancestors he calls "the American" that put the entire relationship between us into an entirely new framework. If I were the ancestor and he my descendant, this helped to create the possibility of causality. The question was: Why? Why did this adventure begin to occur?

This question is explored in some depth in the first three Spiritwalker books, in which it is posited that these periodic visionary connections seemed to be activated in response to similar events experienced in his time and my own simultaneously, whatever *simultaneous* means under such circumstances; and yet within these connections, there was always more, much more.

Because the entirety of an episode occurs in an expanded state of awareness, this produces an enhanced experience of everything—the edges as well as the center —creating a multilevel montage. When I am in connection with him, it's as though I exist on several different levels of reality at the same time—physical, mental, emotional, and spiritual. What seems problematic for some of my readers is that my personal visionary experiences include revelations about a time in which everything that we all take so much for granted in our world is gone – yet not *quite* everything.

Many people have asked me if this is the only potential future available to us. I usually answer that I feel there are limitless futures available, and that the ones that will come into being will be determined by the actions and decisions we make now, in the present time. And yet as we consider the state of our world today, the possibility of a collapse looms on the horizon, and Nainoa's world could well be the future that we're walking straight into if we continue to do business as usual.

Some have called these visions apocalyptic, and some consider them to be in the realm of prophecy. In that regard, let me say that I have absolutely no intention or ego investment in going in that direction. If my visions are true reflections of a future time, we will experience that directly. No escape.

Still others regard what was seen in the visions with deep reassurance. I seem to have had a glimpse into a future world that many discern to be considerably more appealing than the one we live in right now. It is also of interest to my inner scientist that all the educated predictions I made about climate change more than 25 years ago in those first three Spiritwalker books are happening now — and just as fast as I thought they might. This causes pause for more thought.

What I saw and experienced in my visions always seemed to be balanced by an extraordinary complex set of revelations about the nature of ourselves, about what we are all doing here in our sequential lifetimes, and about our destiny as souls traveling across eternity. And this subject matter is not inconsiderable, as many decades ago it caught the attention of the esteemed psychologist C. G. Jung.

In addition, this book is not derived from any one cultural perspective or branch of spirituality. Rather, it presents insights that may be derived from *many* mystic paths, if one chooses to walk them with humility, reverence, and self-discipline. It's about being a twisted hair, weaving many traditions back into the one.

With these leading thoughts, I can, with some hesitation, share with you, the reader, something of what I've learned, something of what I've seen and heard. And when I consider who I used to be before these experiences began, this is not a small thing, to be sure.

So let us begin, and I will now attempt to create a multilayered fabric of narrative—an account created largely by this man Nainoa, with his own perceptions of the world as it exists in the Museum of Time, as well as his insights derived from his experiences of our world and time as perceived through me. The challenge will be to try to record it all through *his* cultural perspective. I believe I am up to this challenge.

That said, let me note that with the 2001 publication of my third book, *Visionseeker*, my ongoing connections with Nainoa slowly ceased, and I came to assume that they were never to continue.

Then one morning in June 2010, in a hotel room near a freeway in California, a powerful state of sleep paralysis overcame me. Similar to what I've described in my earlier books, I found myself back in connection with Nainoa after almost a ten-year hiatus. We've been in periodic relationship since that reconnection, and during this time, I've learned much and shared much as well.

Since so many of my book's readers have asked me for more about Nainoa and his world, I've decided to engage in an experiment, for that is what scientists do. There is never a guarantee of success, and yet this one seems worthy, built on a strong experiential foundation. I have encouraged *Nainoa* to write this book, the one I am calling *Timeweaver: The Book of Nainoa.*

In this regard, allow me to add a translator's note. Nainoa speaks a language unknown today, yet as a former clerk educated by his adoptive father, who was also a clerk, he is well versed in what he calls the classics—those preserved books and manuscripts of The Great Age that were written and rewritten across the intervening millennia by former clerks using the language his people know as Old English. This is not the Old English of Chaucer's time. From Nainoa's perspective, it is the old language we know today as modern English.

The narrative that follows includes Nainoa's thoughts and narratives created for my benefit, including episodes of his life that I experienced in his present time, as well as narratives drawn from his memories of what has transpired. I will periodically insert my own thoughts and reactions, as noted by my initials, *HW*, and such inclusions in the narrative are meant to clarify, categorize, or even enhance what Nainoa has conveyed.

He has recorded some of this in written form in old English, yet when we are in connection, I can also understand the gist of what he's thinking, saying, or experiencing in his own language. This is easier to experience than it is to describe. It just happens. As you, the reader, might be able to appreciate, this took some getting used to in the beginning. But in response, the richness of our relationship and what I've learned from Nainoa has been extraordinary.

So, Nainoa's book will be transmitted by him and transcribed through me, and my job will be to try to get it down right. Let's see what he has to say. . .

Hank Wesselman,
Honaunau, Hawai'i

THE BOOK OF NAINOA

INTRODUCTION

My name is Nainoa Kaneohe, and I am descended from esteemed ancestors in the Kaneohe family who were among those who migrated from the home islands of what was once called Hawai'i to the western coasts of what was once known as America. The voyagers arrived on the coast of this continent in a large fleet of ocean-going canoes eight generations ago—almost 180 years of linear time—and they established communities around the edge of what we call the Inland Sea. My ancestor, the one I call "the American," believes that this was once a great central valley in what was known as California, which is now filled with a marine inundation.

Although the true nature of my ancestry was unknown to me in the earlier part of my life, much has been made of my long walk into the interior of the lost continent of America and my discovery of the Ennu people, as well as my finding horses living east of the mountains—a geographic barrier that separates the great lowland forests that surround the Inland Sea to the west from the comparatively drier interior with its many lakes and wooded grasslands in the east. The American has written about this in his other books.

This adventure changed my life considerably. Upon my departure, I was a servant, a clerk in service to the High Chief of my land division. Upon my return a year later, the High Chief revealed the story of my ancestry and my relationship to his family. In response to my discoveries on my long walk, I was elevated to "Chiefly" status of no particular rank—a Noa Chief free of any cultural restrictions.

In addition, my growing abilities as a spiritual healer, fostered by an Ennu elder I named William the Hunter, who returned with me from the east, led to my being inducted into the Order of Kahuna, a fellowship of philosophers, healers, and wisdom keepers, both women and men. Needless to say, this was and is quite an honor. I continue to learn from them, and I enjoy their great good company whenever we meet.

One of these worthies with whom I have a close heart connection is my father-in-law, High Chief Wilipaki. This leads me to add that my social rank has been elevated enormously by my marriage to his daughter, High Chiefess Maraea Kahalopuna, who, upon the passing of her grandmother, High Chiefess Ruth Kahalopuna, has become the current Governor of all the land divisions around the Inland Sea. This reveals that I am the consort to the Governor, and lest this sound overly political, allow me to add that Maraea and I first met during our childhood when we became close friends. Upon meeting her again more than ten years ago, our former friendship deepened into an intense and enduring "lovership," and we married, an account that has been recorded in my own writings and those of the American as well.

As I reflect now on my journey into the continental interior and its aftermath, there is another element that is quite extraordinary, for it was during my crossing of the great lowland forests that I began to have spiritual visions. As they continued, I slowly became aware that my mind had been drawn into connection in some mysterious way with spirits on the one hand, and with the mind and soul of another man on the other. This man lived in the remote past; this is the one I call the American, who resided in the home islands of Hawai'i and also in California in the time before the Fall.

Through our occasional and extraordinarily vivid connections across the dreamtime, I learned much about this man and his world, as did he about mine, and I slowly began to suspect that he was one of my ancestors and that this was part of the cause for our connection. Once established, our meetings across time continued to deepen, becoming an ongoing continuum during my long walk and its aftermath. To say that I was surprised by this would be an understatement. I was wonderstruck, for this man was much like me—a scholar like myself—and his home was filled with books, his mind and memories filled with knowledge.

Such a resource! For a period of time, I was able to access this man's mind through our entangled dreaming, and from him I recovered vast amounts of lost knowledge from the remote past. Some of this information about what he calls the high technology of his time is extraordinarily complex and almost impossible to understand, yet the American is also a historian, as I am, and his knowledge of the history of Earth and its life forms and peoples is unparalleled even among our own wisdom keepers.

And the time in which he lived? I know from our own archives that the Fall—the collapse of the great American civilization—occurred perhaps 250 generations ago or possibly more. My ancestor, considering each generation to be about 25 years, believes that we are separated by between 5- and 6,000 years.

The cause of his culture's collapse has been one of my preoccupations for much of my life, and through the American, I have been able to learn much about the conditions that may have contributed to the Fall. As I continued to seek information through him about his time, mysteriously the connection between us slowly ceased, creating a period of silence that has lasted for about ten seasonal cycles. During this time, I have thought often about this and have felt great regret that it was over, whatever it had been.

One night, I received a brief pulse of contact with him, then more silence. And then several years ago, I was able to reestablish the connection through my focused concentration and for a specific reason, but that is part of the account that follows. Let me say here that our relationship has now been mysteriously reestablished, at least for a period of time, and my ancestor has posed an unusual request of me. He has proposed that I write a record about the past years of my life—the period that occurred during the time of silence between us.

In response to the books that he created about our connections during my long walk, it seems that the people of *his* time wish to know more about me and *my* time. So the American has extended a proposal to me— that I write this book, and that he, through accessing my efforts across the spiritual plane of dreaming, will transcribe my book into his version of what we call Old English. This means that as I write the account that follows, he will access it, or parts of it, and create his own version of my narrative, and then make it available to his own people through what he calls "published form."

This will be an extraordinary endeavor for both of us, to say the least, yet I feel compelled to accept the American's challenge and follow his lead, for he and his culture appear to be in a race against time, a race in which his civilization (and his life) will come to an end. He seems to be living in one of those magical windows between one cycle of ages and the next, when he believes that his people can either step up toward who and what they are destined to become and create, or they can step back into the cultural complex that he calls *barbarism.*

I am not sure what this means, so in the account that follows, I will share something of our respective lives and times as well as the nature of how they are interconnected. In doing so, it is my hope that the severity of change in his time and place will be mitigated, and that he and his culture will continue, at least for a while.

Ali'i Nainoa Kaneohe,
    Kahalopuna Land Division

1

THE SANCTUARY

Where to begin?

I am alone, sitting cross-legged on a stack of woven mats next to a low writing table. I have been in deep meditation, watching the omnipresent flow of memory, mind stuff, and dreams as they pass through my consciousness. I smile. I've gotten better with practice at keeping them distinct.

The smell of woodsmoke drifts in the late-afternoon air from the cooking fires of the sprawling capitol below. Birdcalls hover in the silence. I smile again. The one I call the American describes my ongoing thoughtlines as mental television. Despite his attempts to describe what television was—a machine that produced pictures, I still lack a foundation from which to understand such abstract knowledge.

Abruptly, I sense that familiar presence nested within my mind now, that curious feeling that belies my connections with this interesting man across what he calls the space-time continuum. As I consider the implications of this, I crack open my eyes and peer through the dim light of my sanctuary. This is my personal *heiau* [temple] located high above my familial compound in which I reside with my lady, High Chiefess Maraea, and our two daughters when she is in residence. Also residing there is Maraea's heart sister and cousin, High Chiefess Kaonokianalu (Nalu), and her son. There are, as well, all of our staff and servants and their families—more than 100 people in all—although many of the children are being raised by their grandparents in the town.

With the passing of both her grandmother and her mother, Maraea became the Governor of all the land divisions around the Inland Sea. As a result, our compound has grown, and the singular guesthouse below my own cottage has now tripled, with another already in construction. Guests are now a part of my political and personal life as the husband of the Governor. Needless to say, my life has become quite complicated. I think about this, and my smile turns into a grimace. Politics is not my preferred area of operation. Maraea is good at it, however. She is a gifted leader, and this gives me a certain degree of freedom.

I unroll a large sheet of finely crafted paper on my desk and block it with stones to keep it flat. Much time has passed since I have last taken a finely crafted calligraphic brush to paper. I glance at the stack of large, sealed timber bamboo tubes arranged in honeycomb-like shelving along one wall. They preserve my original handwritten manuscript of my long walk into the interior of the American continent and the aftermath of this journey so many years ago. This account has been transcribed by a cluster of trained clerks throughout many of the land divisions, providing copies that are now archived into the libraries of most of the Chiefly ruling families around the Inland Sea. I think of them as *books*; the American calls them *scrolls*.

In response to my own book of the events that transpired on that journey, members of the citizenry of our communities began to look toward me as a source of leadership, knowledge, and also spiritual power. I now serve as a counselor and adviser to virtually all the Chiefly families in the varied land divisions.

The locations of their landholdings are determined by accessible bays for maritime activity, abundant freshwater sources and arable soils, and landforms suitable for agriculture and animal husbandry. I grew up in such a land division, where I was a clerk to the High Chief John Kaneohe, so I am conversant with each and every aspect of administering a large agricultural estate. This knowledge allows me to function at the highest levels of estate administration. As I have mentioned, it was also revealed to me years ago that I am related to the Kaneohe family. This was through my grandfather, a High Chief of great spiritual power who misused that gift and whose name is never mentioned. Yet he was a mystic, and my descendant relationship to him seems to have conveyed a degree of his spiritual power to me.

The mystics in my society are highly regarded, as they carry great personal *mana* [power] as well as *'ike* [spiritual ability and knowledge]. They are able to use their minds and their bodies to create bridges between themselves and the Dreaming of Nature, as well as the Dreaming of the Higher Intelligences above. Some become powerful healers. These skills are possessed by only a few, and yet the ability seems to have been exercised by my ancestor. This gift is all-important in maintaining balance and equilibrium within the community on the one hand, as well as between the community and the powers of Nature, the Life Force, and the Ancestors on the other. I appear to be one of these worthies who possesses this gift.

I consider the brush I am holding and unstopper my ink. So where to begin?

2

THE HALE MUA

I OPEN the gate and step up onto the long lanai that borders the outside of my cottage. Entering, I untie and hang the *malo* [loincloth] I wear most of the time on one of the wooden hooks set into the wall. I wash my face and hands in a bowl of water. My living space is simple—a wide, raised platform bed along one side of the single room, with many layers of flat, woven mats covered with cotton blankets and pillows stuffed with silk floss from the seed pods of the great cotton trees in the forest. The floor is paved with closely set smooth stones, and in the room's center is a firepit recessed into the floor, also lined with stones. The far wall bears wooden shelving for my folded clothing. There is also a stool and a wooden table bearing various possessions, including two flat stone lamps with one bamboo container of wicks and a wooden bowl of kukui oil to burn for light. There are also writing materials.

I glance up at the underside of the thick thatch roof and observe the wooden crossbeams blackened by smoke. My cottage is always fragrant with the scent of woodsmoke. Two small high windows in the roof's peaked ends can be opened with a pole to let the smoke out. Windows in the walls on both sides of my house are covered with woven slat screens that can be propped open with long sticks for cross breezes.

I think about the living space of the American that I have seen through my visionary contacts with him. His house is large and composed of many rooms, all filled with objects and beds and chairs and books—many shelves of books. What a resource! I reflect on all I have been able to recover from the past through his mind. I have been able to bring back lost knowledge of many things that have enriched my life and the lives of all the people living in the land divisions around the Inland Sea in the past years.

I run a wooden comb through my black hair, which is now turning gray at the sides, and my beard too. I tie back my hair into a style the American calls a *ponytail*, then don a yellow cloak and a set of matching yellow baggy trousers died with olena root. I drink from a wooden cup filled with water and then let myself out to walk down the paved path to the *hale mua*, the large round men's house with a peaked thatch roof. To one side of the path is a channel lined with stones to carry off the water of heavy rains.

I study the building as I approach because I designed

it. Seen from above from the perspective of a parrot flying over, there would actually be two round houses, the men's on this side and the women's on the other. Between the two are the open-air kitchens that serve both. Those are sheltered from the rains by another circular thatch roof.

I step into the men's side, and as I thread my way through the benches and tables, I am greeted by many of my staff and servants who exchange news and views. My progression toward my accustomed table on the raised platform at one end of the large room is slow. I pass by the kitchens and glance in and greet the cooks, all of whom are men. Finally I sit, and I am served by a young boy whom I know well. My wooden bowl contains a mound of steaming beans and several slabs of sweet plantain, cooked in palm oil until they are orange, with a dollop of spicy salsa on top made of onions, tomatoes, and hot peppers. Rounding it out is a small slab of roasted goat meat.

I inhale the scents of the food with appreciation, sprinkle a pinch of sea salt on the meat, and eat it first. Then I stir the salsa into the beans with my bamboo *hashi* [chopsticks], savoring the sweetness of the plantains with the hotness of the peppers and beans. The boy brings me a bamboo cup filled with water.

I glance through the kitchens into the women's house on the other side. There, I catch a glimpse of Chiefess Nalu with a clutch of children at her table on a raised platform similar to my own, revealing them as persons of rank. The children include both of my daughters with

Maraea as well as my son with Nalu. She catches my eye and smiles widely. Maraea is still in residence at the Governor's mansion, involved with affairs of state, as she often is these days. *Maybe tonight,* I think.

My older daughter, Elika Kahalopuna, and her sister, Ana, spot me and bolt through the adjoining doors, running up to me and hugging me as I laugh and rub their little backs, whispering funny things in their ears. I love them so. Then they kiss me quickly on the cheek and run back into the women's house, rejoining Nalu and their half-brother. I hear Nalu's laugh and see the flash of her smile. Our son is still young and somewhat shy. He is thoughtful and doesn't miss much. We share a smile.

As I dig into my dinner with a sigh, I reflect on our custom of men and women eating separately. I have learned from my ancestor that this was an ancient *kapu* [sacred directive] that had been broken in the remote past, creating great misfortune for the Hawaiian peoples of that time. No one knew for sure why the custom had been broken or later reassumed, although there were many theories. It was known, however, that the ramifications of the broken kapu had been severe, and now men and women ate separately once again unless circumstance demanded a rescinding of the directive. And this did happen from time to time for ceremonial reasons. A warm memory emerges in my mind of the feast of celebration when Maraea and I became husband and wife—an event that has been described in the American's earlier books.

I had accepted this cultural separation between the

male and female sectors of my society uncritically, and my family compound reflected this, its entirety being divided into the women's half and the men's half. The women lived together with their dependent children on their side, and the men lived on theirs, with visitations between husbands and wives usually in the residences in the men's half, but not always. When the boys came of age, they moved into the men's half to live with their fathers. Our social world is liquid and free-flowing, as my ancestor would say. Yet the world of men and the world of women is quite separate, each with its own focus and work, the two coming together in the nexus of the family.

My thoughts are interrupted as various members of the community approach me, sharing issues of concern on the one hand or appreciation on the other. I know them all—their ancestral names, their current family names, and their children's names. I am the Chief of this community, and I sit in the chair of responsibility. That means that the well-being of everyone in my compound is my concern—from my immediate family to my extended family of servants; from the highest to the lowest; from my wives and children and my personal advisers to the servants, street sweepers, gardeners, and dung carriers and their families. I know them all, and I care for them, and they love my family and me as well. I briefly consider the shape of my own family in response to these thoughts.

To be the husband of the Ali'i Nui Maraea Kahalopuna, the Governor of all the land divisions, is not a small thing. We now have two children together, daughters we named after my ancestor's children. Then there is Nalu, Maraea's cousin, chief confidant, and heart sister, as well as the mother of a son by me—named Henele after the American (whose birth name was Henry). Senior wife and junior wife – this is how it is now. I had never considered this social form as different until I connected with my ancestor.

In the American period, the social convention for a family was that of one husband, one wife, and their dependent children—a curious arrangement, I think, and one that created separation, perhaps. In my own time, men and women can love whom they wish, with respectful observance of social decorum, political connections, and genealogical lineages . . . and with occasional lapses. This usually works well, but not always, and several problematic relationship issues arise in my mind.

My ruminations are interrupted as High Chief Wilipaki comes into the hall. A close relationship has formed between us over the years. And how could it not? Wilipaki is Maraea's father. He is also a kahuna mystic and a visionary.

We greet each other warmly with the *honi*, pressing our noses and faces together to share the sacred breath of life, the *ha*. The elder kahuna joins me at my table, where he is served his own bowl of food. Then Wilipaki digs in and chews thoughtfully. "Your cooks are very good, Nainoa. Who would have known that beans and plantains combined would make such a succulent feast? And the goat meat is tender. . .."

I smile and say, "It is a dish I acquired from my ancestor, who lived for a time among the peoples in the fabled lands of Africa. This recipe came from there."

Wilipaki observes me with acute focus for long moments; then he smooths back his brushy mustache and beard and keeps on eating. "Very good." A servant brings us both wooden cups of rum as well as water for Wilipaki.

We toast each other and drink the fiery liquid, and I reflect again on how much I have learned from my ancestor about many things, including ceramics. From him I have acquired the knowledge of earthen sediments, the ones he calls clays. Also from him I have learned how to gather these clays, and how they can be shaped in coils to rise as pots and then smoothed and dried, and then fired in our earth ovens to create bowls in which food may be cooked or served, with smaller bowls made for eating, and still smaller bowls for drinking, although I still prefer my wooden food bowl and cup.

I watch Wilipaki eat and think about those places the American calls *sites*, such as the *siti* [city] site I visited at the onset of my long walk into the interior of the continent. I have organized large parties of commoners to find and dig into these sites. At large ones we create what the American calls a satellite community with charcoal burners, hunters, construction workers to build houses, foresters to fell trees, and others. In doing so, we have recovered much, including many large pots made of metal. All were covered by a skin of white substance that when removed with abrasive river sand allowed them to turn silvery and take up their original function—cooking food. My ancestor calls this metal *aluminum*.

In my kitchens I have a collection of such pots, including the large ones we use for preparing food over wood-burning stoves made of stacked stone that I designed to support them. Our traditional earth ovens are in a separate open-air building where we roast and smoke meat. Long tables for food preparation and wooden barrels of drinking water and smaller ones of rum are also present in the kitchens. The walls at each end support wooden shelving for the storage of food bowls and utensils.

The recovery of these metal pots over the past years has created quite a sensation and has encouraged other ruling families in other land divisions to send their workers into the forests around the Inland Sea to find other sites. The mining of these scattered places has yielded more of this silvery metal, and as a result, the metalworkers of our communities are doing a brisk business.

I wonder, as always, if I can recover the knowledge of how to mine metals directly from the earth, as this skill was lost with the Fall of the American's civilization and the subsequent isolation of our home islands. My ancestor has been advising me as to what he calls the "technical processes of metallurgy." He had seen metals being smelted by men in the fabled lands of Africa, and I already had sketches that revealed how to build a small oven (kiln) of clay and stone and stack it with alternate layers of charcoal and scrap metal, as well as stones with metal in them.

I had learned that this mixture could be ignited, and then the fierce heat would do its work and release the metal. Then the oven could be broken open and the raw metal scraped from the embers. Our metalworkers had adapted the knowledge I had received and had created similar ways, using more charcoal as well as bellows to reheat and shape the metal.

In this regard, the American has suggested that the red stained earth at the ruined siti sites might be mined for metals in this way. He also revealed that there may be localities in the Ennu lands to the east, places where metal ores might be located, extracted, and processed. In his time, he has access to such knowledge.

During one of our connections, I asked the American how to locate metals in the earth. He informed me that in an ancient time during which metals had first been discovered and worked, there were what he called *ores*, metals in stones that were easily accessible on the earth. But with the great demand for metals in his time, these ores on or near the surface were quickly exhausted, and a form of high technology was created to extract them from deep within what he calls "the earth's crust." That knowledge and technology was lost with civilization's Fall and likely would never be recovered, as it would involve the necessity of using large machines designed for the purpose, already made of metal.

HW:

I'm always amazed by how much Nainoa has been able to extract from my memory banks, such as my early attempts to work with pottery long ago in my younger years. The knowledge of smelting metals from ore came from my memories of West Africa, where I was a Peace Corps volunteer in the 1960s. And it was during my years in Africa that I continually encountered metalworkers in sprawling open-air markets who were shaping metal tools over charcoal fires enhanced by assistants using portable bellows.

In the next passage, Nainoa reveals something about what an individual—trained in the ability to memorize information and records of all kinds—can do. It happened during his meal with Wilipaki.

3

CONTACT

MY RECONNECTION with the American began on a subsequent excursion into the forests east of the Inland Sea, where I was involved in a major project. I will write more about this later. On that night, I was wrapped in my cloak in my hammock near the banks of the river that my fellow explorers and I had been following, and was almost asleep when the deep, mystical state suddenly presented itself. The intense physical pressure gripped me, and after the customary visual perceptions of the great luminous grid and spots of light, the connection was established, and I was there.

My awareness was merged with the mind and body of the American in the usual way. This time I heard a strange pulsating, roaring noise. I was able to determine that the man was in bed and half-asleep, and he was dreaming. He slowly emerged in response to my presence.

"Warm greetings, esteemed ancestor," I said in Old English, accompanied by a hiss of swirling energy.

"Warm greetings in return, esteemed descendant," he responded sleepily, with another ongoing hiss. Then he said something curious: "Long time no see . . ." and indeed, the period of silence had lasted many years.

My vision came up as the American's eyes opened to survey a dark room with a large bed, and his wife, Jill, asleep to one side. The windows were covered with what appeared to be blankets (curtains), yet light was slipping through their edges. The strange rushing sounds were coming from without. In response to my curiosity, his thoughts took form. *Cars*, came his thought. *Road*. I digested this. I had seen the great roads of his time and their wagons powered by machines through his eyes before. I gathered my own thoughts and expressed them for our mutual consideration.

"I require information about wild horses. I need to know about them and how their society is organized. I wish to be able to make contact with the horse ancestor so that I can connect and interact with the horses in the Ennu lands. I must discover how best to approach them since they have been hunted by the Ennu and are understandably wary. I wish to capture an entire herd, and I must learn how to do that and how to gentle them so that we can bring them back through the great forest of the lowlands to our communities. We wish to breed and raise them in the land divisions around the Inland Sea.

"Since you are a scholar, as I am, I wonder if you can

access this information and provide it to me so that I may succeed in this great endeavor. I know that you were raised in a great siti without horses, but perhaps you can help me. In your own time, horses were still in service to human beings. I need to know how this can be accomplished once again."

As the American came fully awake, he began to think. I followed his thoughts, and something unexpected appeared on the "screen," as he would say.

Horses live in dry, open, grassy country, he thought. *They do not live in forests or in forested environments. It may be that the heavy rains around the Inland Sea create wetlands that will not be good for their hooves. Then there is the grass that they eat. . .*

The American paused in his thoughts and then added: *Your intentions to capture horses and tame them may require that they become part of new communities that you first establish in the interior. Then see what is possible in your land divisions if your people construct shelters (stables) for them and clear enough land to create grassy meadows for grass. But the horses eat a lot of grass.*

Then I felt the connection slipping, for some reason, and within a heartbeat, it was gone. I had expressed my wish, my intention, and the American had received it. Now the only thing I could do was wait for the next one.

I sit at my writing desk now, recalling that contact. This was the beginning of our reconnection, brief as it was. I marvel as always at the intensity as well as the nature of these vivid encounters. And that night I was too excited to sleep.

4

———

THE SPIRIT STONE

I PAUSE in this writing and glance up at the two windows nestled under the roof's peak. Both ends of the small rectangular wood-and-stone structure is fitted into the rock outcrop above my compound. A light evening rain has begun to patter on the thick thatch of the roof. To my left, a low altar spans the room, bearing in its center the spirit stone *Kapohakuki'ihele*—The Stone That Travels. The upright dark-lava slab was the stone of my ancestors, brought on a great double-hulled voyaging canoe from the home islands more than eight generations ago. Before it, sits a flat stone kukui oil lamp with several wicks alight. There is also a wooden bowl of water in which floats a red flower from the garden as an offering.

The spirit that resides within this stone came into relationship with me at the beginning of my long walk when it informed Chief Kaneohe that it wanted to meet me. The connection deepened on my return, and when my

19

kinsman passed into the company of his ancestors some years ago, the spirit stone came into my stewardship in accordance with the High Chief's wishes.

I stare thoughtfully at the large black stone, observing its rather grim visage with affection. It—or the spirit that resides within it—has played a major role in my life, perhaps serving as an ongoing link between the American and me. The stone seems to enable, as well, links into the various levels of the Dreaming of the Spiritual Worlds. And now, as I feel the presence of the American nested within my mind, I marvel, as always, at the role the spirit stone is playing in this interesting relationship. I smile as I realize that this is part of the story that needs to be told, a quest that began many cycles ago, and one that forever changed my life, as well as the life of my ancestor. *And can stones do that?* I wonder?

"That and more." A memory of a voice within my mind answers me and continues. "For stones do not have to think about anything. Stones simply know." It is the voice of William the Ennu, Kenojelak's father and an accomplished spiritwalker from beyond the great mountains east of the Inland Sea.

And what do stones know? I ask. The answer comes quickly into my mind in the Ennu language: "The stones possess the story of the Universe and much more." I think about this.

The spirit stone was still in the care of High Chief Kaneohe when I married High Chiefess Maraea and moved into her life in the capitol in the Kahalopuna Land division. Now that the stone is close to me once again, my connection with the American seems to be starting up again as well. I look at the stone thoughtfully. *And what of my ancestor,* I wonder?

A pause, then a thought comes, and whether it is my thought or that of my ancestor, I am not sure. Perhaps the past connections between the two of us occurred when the American was in proximity to the spirit stone, as I was myself, at least in the beginning, for the American was the one who had found it by a bay on Hawai'i Island, and he was the one who carved it. He had been the first caretaker of the stone.

I consider this and wonder if it is the nature of the Mystery within all things to remain ever elusive, beckoning us forward, ever forward, toward that which we can never quite grasp. *Perhaps,* I think, *the Mystery draws us toward that which we are destined to become.* This means I have to trust that the spiritual forces with whom the American and I seem to be aligned have a plan, projecting us forward on the path upon which we agreed to walk before we were born.

But again, I think, *that is part of the story that remains to be written.* I smile as the words appear in my mind. I consider the implications of this thought, and the flow within my mind takes an interesting turn, one I am sure is not my own. There is an impulse coming through—one that confirms the desire to create this book. I sit very still and consider this. Then comes a request. *There is also Kenojelak—what has happened to her?* My blood quickens as I think of her. My ancestor wants to know about her. And how could he not? The American had been there when I had come into relationship with my Ennu wife, many years ago. And yes, I must write about my reconnections with her.

I emerge from my contemplations, and my eyes sweep my surroundings again. Years ago, I had altered the wide and largely flat rocky ledge on the hillside, enlarging it and terracing it; and with a contingency of skilled stoneworkers, I had created his small personal sanctuary, this heiau as my personal place of power. When I am in residence in the capitol, I sit here in light meditation every morning and evening. It is here that I shall write this book.

I close my eyes once again. I feel the presence of the forest around me and the awareness of the spirit stone, in addition to the presence of the other that I perceive within myself. A merging occurs in which all becomes a singularity that I embody, and all is good. I watch my thoughts as they expand.

Then . . . the bell sounds from my compound below. It is a flat slab of wood, suspended from a house beam and struck with a wooden mallet. Emerging from my thoughts, I put down brush and ink and leave the fresh roll of handmade paper blocked with stones. I look through the door. It is twilight. *Tomorrow,* I think, *and now for some dinner.* And just maybe I will be graced later this evening by the presence of my lady, Maraea, or her kinswoman, lady Nalu.

I glance again at the stone, then place my hand on it for long moments, feeling its roughness and our connection. The stone feels warm. I blow out the wicks of the lamp with a blessing and stand, stretching out my joints. Stooping, I emerge from the small door of the heiau. The light rain had stopped as soon as it had begun.

For long moments I just stand alone on the ledge in the glimmering light. Below, I can see the town beyond my compound, a sprawling mass of houses radiating out from the center in ever-growing circles. Most of the houses have thatch roofs, and some have wooden shingles. The woodsmoke is rising through holes in their roofs as firewood burns for the evening meal. And on many, the smoke simply flows through the thatch, giving the impression that the extensive community is smoldering.

I inhale the breath of the damp forest; then I descend the wet stone steps through a gathering mist. The hazy moon is just rising through the clouds in the east, and long columns of fruit bats are flying toward some destination that they know will provide sustenance. As I pause and watch them, the screech of a long-tailed parrot rings from the forest. My ancestor calls them *macaws*. Then I resume my descent, and emerging from the fog with wisps of mist still clinging to me, I walk back into my world.

5

A TRANSMISSION FROM THE PAST

MY RUMINATIONS CEASE as Wilipaki takes a large swig of his rum and looks at me with affection. "And what is occurring between the two of you now, if I may ask? Between you and your ancestor? I am aware that you receive information about his time and place through him."

I observe the elder uneasily and consider my response as I take a long draw from my own cup of rum. He has always had a high degree of what my ancestor calls *psychic ability*, and he has obviously been listening in to my thoughts.

"As you know, my connection with the American is sporadic; it is 'on again, off again,' as he would say. It has been off for a long time, but right now it appears to be coming 'on again,' and in response, something very interesting has been revealed.

"In his early elderhood, my ancestor fell into relationship with a revered Hawaiian kahuna named Hale Makua during the last years of this man's life. Makua was a mystic who shared some of his traditional wisdom with the American and his wife. This included handwritten accounts of the kahuna's transmissions received from his ancestors while in meditation. The American has been committing this knowledge to memory, and when we are in contact, large sections of this body of wisdom can be transmitted directly to me. It is as though I can absorb this *mana'o* [wisdom] directly through the connection we have with each other."

I stop talking and look at the elder sitting across from me, watching for his response. "My ancestor calls these *transmissions*. I'm not sure which word would be appropriate in Old Hawaiian, perhaps *ho'ili* or *ho'ouna*. When the connections happen, the information all arrives together, mixed up into one common hash." The two of us laugh. "Then I have to figure it all out." We laugh again.

I continue. "Here is an example of what I have received recently, which reveals the depth of the old Hawaiian kahuna's knowledge as well as his trust in the American." I sit back and close my eyes. Long moments pass as I access this information, and then the words come and I begin to speak. "These are, or were, the kahuna's words in Old English. My ancestor communicated this passage directly from the elder Hawaiian. It was as though the entire narrative was transferred to my mind from his when we were in connection. This one is of meaning to me, as we seem to be starting a new series of connections."

Makua's Words

In all true beginnings, there is no knowledge of what will follow. And in the beginning, we have no real understanding of what it means to walk the spiritual path, for our lives have yet to be tested against the stark reality of the enormous changes and challenges that life will present to us.

Yet we discover along the way that there is a constant dialogue between the physical and nonphysical worlds, and this can be both frightening as well as illuminating—even thrilling. This is because the direct experience of interdimensional communication presents us with the possible levels of guidance that are advanced, both in scope as well as intention.

We come to realize that we are meant to work with a dimension of life that is far greater than that which can only be seen or appreciated in physical form. We come to understand that humankind is a collective body responsible not only for the quality of life on Papa Hanau Moku *[Earth], but equally responsible to the Universe for the quality of the thoughts and actions affecting the* te mauri ora *[life force]. And it is through this collective planetary interaction that we all discover how important and precious each of us is to the greater spectrum of life.*

The knowledge of our indissoluble connectedness to all life is the true beginning, and though our lives have been filled with many opportunities and challenges before meeting each other, our real learning began with our first encounter. With the passage of time, we come to deeply appreciate the nature and power of choice as well as the inevitability of change. Nothing ever remains the way it was. We change, our work changes, our friends change, and every aspect of our life changes.

Along the way, we discover that life in all its beautiful and challenging aspects has shifted into a new pattern, a new cycle. And in this time, with or without guidance from the expanded realms, our life lessons continue, often touching us deeply where we are most vulnerable. We discover in response to such life lessons that there is no substitute for such learning. Our lessons seem to be offered to us in relation to the issues we most need to see clearly. And in response, we are led into the inner realms of our lives that are spiritual in nature.

These inner dimensions—though very private and very tender—are also amazingly persistent in drawing our attention back to our own true self and to the special qualities that are ours alone. The inner worlds offer solace and healing energy necessary for us to grow into our personal empowerment.

In response, we are encouraged to reevaluate our lives and are urged through our inner stirrings to move in strange and unfamiliar directions. And this, in turn, gives us the opportunity to grow. As we move beyond those seemingly safe places and belief systems, we enter the unknown, where we eventually encounter universal wisdom and understanding as well as the love that has carried us through our most vigorous and painful of journeys.

Change, as we know, is the texture of the Universe that is in no way punitive or disciplinary, but rather growth producing and creative. The state of change is permanent and continually directs our attention toward that on which we can depend—toward that which is true versus that which is transient. It is in this way that all forms of life come to appreciate their primary relationship to the greater Universe.

In this manner, we also come to value the physical life reality and get to see it for what it is: transient. When we consciously form our thoughts into intentions, and our intentions into appropriate actions, this allows us to live life to our fullest capacity, existing for our own greatest good. And it is then that we may turn toward the spirit teachers in the expanded realms of consciousness in order to help us bring into being our full and complete magnificence.

The transmission ceased at this point, and I emerge from my inner focus and pause, then open my eyes. Like myself, Wilipaki is a man educated in the classics that survived from the Great Age. Most were written in Old English, the language of the Americans, to be copied and recopied by clerks across the intervening spans of time, so he understands the gist of what I have just said. He looks thoughtful for long moments, then smiles. "Not bad . . . this kahuna elder was obviously a philosopher."

"Yes, and so was the American . . . like us." I smile in return. "This is the nature of what I am receiving. And often the passages are very long." I laugh. "And in order to remember them, I write them down."

"This is not a small thing to be in connection with spiritual elders from the past," Wilipaki confirms. "It sounds as though both your ancestor and the kahuna were committed to sharing their knowledge with you across time."

I grin and shrug. Wilipaki smiles back. "Now, your job is to get it down and get it right. Not a small thing either when you consider the shape of it. The recovery of lost knowledge from the remote past . . ." Both of us drift into thought, to be interrupted as more members of the community approach with information and with requests for support.

When we are alone again, Wilipaki continues. "We must create some time together, Nainoa. I wish to hear more of these transmissions from the American." Wilipaki pauses and pulls at his beard, now white with age. "And yes, you should write down these transmissions, capturing this kahuna's wisdom from the past." He pauses again. "What an extraordinary thing . . . how *kupaianaha* [wonderful, extraordinary, amazing]!"

We lift our cups of rum and toast each other.

HW:

I was quite amazed by this passage. Years ago, when I wrote Spiritwalker, I became aware that Nainoa was a clerk who had been trained to remember events as well as dialogue in accurate detail. Within his community, only the scholars as well as some among the Chiefly families know how to read and write. In such an essentially oral tradition, much information is stored in the minds of the clerks, especially economic agreements that include the taxes levied on just about everything. Nainoa's talent for total recall is reflected in his rendering of Makua's words, which are essentially just as he wrote them. This required prodigious feats of memory, an ability he'd been trained to acquire since his childhood with Kiwini, his adoptive father who was a clerk.

There's one other thing I want to mention about the metal pots and other artifacts recovered from what Nainoa calls siti sites. *I asked a sculptor friend about the survival of metal objects across 5,000 years. He responded that even corten steel would be gone by then, but that aluminum and bronze would be among the survivors (along with silver and gold, of course), and that aluminum would develop a white patina with age that would protect it. This seems to be the case with Nainoa's pots.*

6

DARK PORTENTS

THE AMERICAN RETURNED to the image-making device on his desk. He did something to it, and what he called the screen went dark. He then sat back in his chair considering what to say to the one (me) nested in his mind. He selected a printed document that was folded into pages from a pile to one side of his table, studied the folios for long moments, then began to think/speak.

"Most of the people who live in my culture today are both troubled and confused. We've achieved great miracles materially and technologically, yet this has not brought us happiness, nor have we been able to envision a future that will bring us ease. Humanity is currently dealing with endless wars, dangerous health epidemics, environmental collapse and famines, as well as political attacks by our leadership upon our fundamental freedoms.

"As you know, a true democracy is based upon

freedom of thought and expression, and it remains the best form of government, yet divisions between the two polarities in our society, progressive and conservative, revolve around a majority and an opposition that are continually in conflict with each other. These divisions are not suited to governing our societies today and are holding back our progression toward a favorable future. We currently have a crisis of leadership at all levels of government.

"The economic situation of our world is completely corrupted, with the most influential networks—powered by immense wealth—essentially enslaving the population. The values of these networks are materialistic and are based on profit and enrichment of the upper rulership of our society. Instead of the economy serving humanity, our citizenry is now in service to the economy. Accordingly, all our nations are dependent on a planet-wide economic system that could be described as totalitarian, a system that utterly neglects the elementary needs of hundreds of millions of people. This means that the wealth generated by our citizens only benefits a small minority among us, a situation that can only be described as deplorable. As in your culture, Nainoa, economics will fulfill its role only when it is serving everybody."

The American paused, and I thought about the information I had just received. He was right, of course. Only when everyone is served and secure can a community thrive. The American was silent, as if considering what to say. Then his thoughtline continued.

"In my time, our technology—the creation of tools and machines to improve our living conditions—has taken up residence in the core of our societies to the extent that it is almost indispensable. Yet there is a dark side to our technological successes, and the development of mechanization has led to the progressive dehumanization of society as machines have replaced people and our communication devices have reduced human contact, creating separation. The problem seems to be that our technology has evolved much faster than our human consciousness. In response, we must respect the quality of life and learn once again, how to live in harmony and balance with Nature as well as with ourselves."

There was a long pause, and then he went on.

"As you are also aware from our frequent contacts in the past, there are five great religions in my time expressing both fundamentalist and progressive movements. They are all currently under siege in response to social change in our time, and if they are to survive, they must discard the most dogmatic moral beliefs and positions they've taken on across many centuries. It is now essential that they adapt to our rapidly changing society and to the times in which we live. In my opinion, most of our problems—cultural and societal—are due to organized religion, and especially regressive religious extremism.

"In addressing the issue of social change, evolution is not a theory; it is a law that the regressive elements in our society reject through a lack of understanding of what the word actually conveys. The law of evolution states that everything changes, including human consciousness and scientific progress; and if poorly educated and strongly opinionated regressives do not understand and accept it, they will condemn themselves to their gradual disappearance, a process that has caused endless religious conflicts. My own presumption is that unless they can modernize their belief systems and faiths, they and their descendants will inevitably disappear.

"The good news is that as our human consciousness continues to grow and expand, the appearance of a universal spiritual complex will become possible, one that will integrate the best that all of our major religious faiths have to offer. In this way, each individual becomes their own priest or priestess, their own teacher or guru, their own prophet, receiving revelations themselves without the need for an organized and hierarchical priesthood to stand between them and their experience of the sacred. The ancient visionary path of the shaman is the ancestor of all our spiritual traditions, and it is reemerging in Western society once again, probably in response to the ease with which the mystic road can be accessed and experienced.

"There is something I learned from my years living with tribal peoples who live in animist societies with shamanist cultural perspectives. Each new generation in such societies had to perpetuate and refresh a continually re-created visionary tradition, even adding to and changing the ever-growing body of knowledge and technique. For it was in this way that the shaman's path of direct revelation remained meaningful and vital for those brave adventurers who walked it. The time has come for fundamentalist belief systems to respect and respond to such sacred knowledge."

The American paused again. I could feel an uplift in his emotional turmoil. Then the shadow returned, and he continued.

"There is the whole matter of our system of education that is now in a state of chaos. Most parents have withdrawn from the educational process of their children, and most lack the qualifications to educate their children themselves. As the emphasis in our educational system has shifted to the teachers of established schools to transmit knowledge, we've neglected the implanting of civic and ethical values. There was a Greek kahuna named Socrates who observed more than 2,000 years before my time that education should be 'the art of awakening the virtues of the soul,' such as kindness, generosity, humility, honesty, and tolerance. These virtues are singularly lacking in my time.

"One of his followers, another Greek kahuna named Plato, was one of democracy's fiercest critics, by the way. He held that to give the vote to the hoi polloi, the masses, was a vast error because they completely lacked the education and the knowledge of how to elect authentic leadership worthy of the task of governance. He felt that only the existing governing leadership had the ability to choose the best from among themselves to govern. As I've mentioned, in my time frame in America, we currently have a serious crisis of leadership on our hands, so perhaps the Greek was right. Our existing leadership is now clearly corrupt and is doing the bidding of the wealthy elite, who are essentially running the show.

"Concerning human relationships, the people of my time have become more and more self-seeking and self-serving; and as I've already mentioned, individuals barely communicate with one another. Our systems of telecommunication have replaced normal in-person social connections, creating ever-increasing separation and placing individuals in isolation, intensifying individualism. The policy of everyone for themselves predominates, a consequence of the excessive materialism rampant in our society. This has also resulted in an overall upsurge in violence. This has always existed, yet it is now increasingly expressing itself, even in children at ever-earlier ages.

"Not only that, but our relationship with Nature has never been so disharmonious, and the corporate businesses in our society are hell-bent on pursuing the short-term economic gain at the expense of long-term environmental sustainability. The monumental waste being generated at all levels of our society is simply appalling.

"We're also faced with corporate entities that are involved with the biological manipulations affecting the food supply in an increasingly negative way, from the widespread use of pollutants to the accumulation of poisonous wastes in our soils, our water, and our air. In this regard, water is an element necessary for the support and maintenance of life; and in my time, access to fresh, uncontaminated water is only available for perhaps one out of six of the world's inhabitants, yet awareness of this peril is lacking in most people today.

"As well, the conditions in which many of our animals are raised and slaughtered for food is appalling. There seems to be no understanding that our behavior toward animals is also part of our relationship with Nature. More than 2,000 years ago, a philosopher among the ancient Greeks observed [the American picked up a printed page], 'As long as men continue to ruthlessly destroy the living beings from the lower kingdoms, they will know neither health nor peace. As long as they massacre animals, they will kill each other, and whoever sows murder and suffering will not and cannot reap joy and love.'"

The American paused, considering what else to say, then stopped before uttering a final thought. His mood was somber.

"As man is a child of the Earth, and Earth a child of the Universe, man is a child of the stars. The Universe and Man need to know each other . . . and this involves respect."

There was silence in his mind then, and he wondered if I had detached. In fact, I was considering all that had been shared. The information was deeply disturbing, and I had begun to understand, as never before, the social and political distortions in the American's society that had led to the collapse of their civilization.

And how did all this come into being? I wondered. In response, the American's mind shifted into the past.

"Before the white people came to what we call North America, all the land was occupied by indigenous peoples, the ones who could be called Amerindians. For thousands of years, they lived in harmony with the land, sharing its bounty with the animals and the birds. They had wars with other tribes, but these were wars fought with honor, and those that were true of heart survived.

"The native peoples never destroyed the land. They took from the land only what was needed, and they gave back as much as they took. Their lifeways blessed the land and its residents . . . and their drums and sacred smoke spoke to the mysteries, the spirits, weaving a harmony between this world and the otherworld. They lived a lifeway that was a path with heart.

"The white people came, and when they arrived, they began a systematic rape of the land. They cleared the forests, butchered the buffalo, and fought the tribes—not in an honorable way, but with genocide. They were 'good' Christians who went to church on Sunday morning and then shot Indians on Sunday afternoon. Over 100 years, 95 percent of the Amerindians were murdered, and their cultures and languages were destroyed.

"The white people bound the land with roads and railways as well as the steel and concrete wastelands we call cities. We fouled the air and created weapons of mass destruction that could destroy vast tracts of countryside and people in a single flash. We waged war in all areas of the world, and we destroyed whole countries and their peoples. In the process, we sacrificed countless numbers of young people in our own military societies for the dreams of old men in the capitols.

"And the indigenous peoples? They were separated from their lands and relegated to reserves that the white people had no use for. And if gold or oil was discovered on those lands, the treaties were ignored, and they were displaced once again. Today they live in abject poverty, unknown in your time, Nainoa.

"We cannot seem to learn from our mistakes. We just keep on making them over and over, and things are not going well."

The intensity and content of the American's thoughts created separation, and our connection simply dissolved like mist. Yet there was that last thought: *Man is a child of the Universe . . .*

I emerge from the deep state and allow my mind to begin to process all that I received. I get out of bed and go to my table, light a lamp, and take brush in hand to record this extraordinary conversation across time. The woman in my bed stirs and turns to look at me.

I look at her with warmth, and smile. "I have been in connection with my ancestor across the dream field. I have received information through him about the time in which he lives, information that will require deep thought."

I remain in deep contemplation for some time, then rise from the bed, wrap a sarong around my waist, and sit down at my writing table again. I guess there will be little sleep for me on this night. I take up the bamboo brush and unstopper my small bamboo container of ink made from burned kukui nut shells, finely ground. I reach for and flatten a prepared role of handmade paper on the table and begin to write.

HW:

This contact occurred some years ago, and although I remember the connection, as well as what was communicated, I have no memory now of the magazine I was reading when I shared my concerns about our current world with Nainoa. Needless to say, those concerns have been amplified in recent years, and I am always impressed by Nainoa's memory skills.

7

CONFLICT RESOLUTION

I COULD NOT SLEEP after transcribing this contact, and after an early breakfast of grilled fish, steamed breadfruit, and coffee in the mua, I ascend to my heiau above my family compound just as the sun is breaking on the horizon. I consider the fresh length of paper on my writing table in the dim light. I unstopper the ink and select a brush, then think about what I wish to record.

I glance at the spirit stone in its dark corner of the room, and I light the oil lamp before it, using a small stone and a fragment of iron from the past to ignite a punk in a large seashell. Then I place my hands on the stone and offer a short prayer and a blessing, adding my gratitude for any role the spirit within it might be playing in my connection with the American.

I think about what I have learned about the state of the society in which the American lived. The disharmony at all levels seems extreme, especially among the governing leadership. I consider our own society around the Inland Sea and how we deal with conflict, for disharmony is always present and needs to be addressed.

I have mentioned the existence of the land divisions into which our society is organized. Each is headed by an ancestral Chiefly family from the home islands and is divided into a maritime community on the coast and an agricultural community extending inland, usually a half day's journey or more between them. There are now many such communities spread out along the shores of the Inland Sea. The leadership of each is composed of a council of wise elders drawn from the order of kahuna, as well as two high Chiefs who have ultimate authority, one on the coast, and one inland.

Every year and in each land division, the farmers, merchants, stock people, craftspeople, and fisherpeople on the coast hold local gatherings where they discuss problems of common concern and settle disputes among themselves. Any unresolved issues are brought before their councils and before their High Chiefs for resolution. Thieves and murderers as well as other criminals are all judged—sometimes with mercy and sometimes without —depending on the offense. Often this involves the cluster of spiritual elders meeting with a large group, usually one or more families, to encourage people to discuss at length their grievances, to speak about their personal contributions to the general disharmony, and to resolve these issues with goodwill.

Everyone respects the presence as well as the guidance of their councils as the elders draw upon their knowledge of the Kanawai, the traditional laws passed down across time, to resolve such issues. To commit these laws to memory often takes ten years or more. It is also true that only the wealthier farmers and fisherpeople have any real presence in the yearly court of justice in the capitol. There are also the commoners who come to support them when they are called upon to do so.

This large gathering is a combination of general socializing in a fairground enhanced by music, food, and drama that creates a kind of spectator sport as each case is presented by specialists who know the ins and outs of the laws that govern us. These worthies are also the ones who present the appeals on behalf of their constituents. There is always the presence as well of a High Chief who serves as a lawgiver. That individual decides on the worthiness of the cases at hand. Also, these learned teachers judge whether the laws have been fairly presented and applied before they are brought before the ultimate authority: the Governor.

As a consequence, the legal presentations often take on the aspect of a drama in which the commoners are given free rein to contribute or not. This assemblage creates a sense of commonality and community at all our societal levels, and this is the manner in which we rule ourselves. Anyone— highborn and commoners alike— can listen to the arguments, conversing among themselves about who is the most skilled at interpreting the laws to support their constituents, and express opinions. And they may offer their own observations.

The inclusion of the commoners' input reveals that our issues and affairs are conducted by the general mass of our citizens as they assemble each year. When the lawgiver speaks, it can often take several days as he or she recites the laws of the Kanawai. The consultation with the spirits of our ancestors by our visionaries is always part of this process. And when the Governor finally casts her judgments, the cases are closed. Thus, the Governor serves as a single wise ruler when need be, and my lady Maraea excels in this role. And how could she not with her father High Chief Wilipaki as adviser and lawgiver?

This reveals that the quality and ethical conviction of our leadership is immensely important, as it maintains and furthers balance and harmony in our society. When I consider what the American has revealed to me about the leadership of his own world, I feel great concern.

I have accompanied High Chief Wilipaki often on his visits to other land divisions where the Chiefs were waiting for him to decide their accumulated legal cases. These were heard in the large reception and banquet hall of each land division, with Wilipaki seated in the chair of authority flanked by his hosts as well as many from the community. They all listened to what the plaintiffs had to say, then called on the defendants for their versions of the events that had transpired. These cases could take many days, during which time Wilipaki usually said little. He listened. When the moment for a judgment arrived, the entire assemblage would wait for his verdict.

Wilipaki would usually refer to similar cases from the past, then would quote the laws that applied. Such was the communities' respect for him as the lawgiver that they never disputed his decisions. Wilipaki's judgments rarely involved physical punishment, but rather focused mainly on compensation, even for the crime of murder. Patiently, Wilipaki listened to each case and decided who was at fault. And when he found that a genuine offense had been committed, he explained its gravity then suggested the correct compensation to be paid.

"Everything depends on the respect that the people have for the Kanawai," he told me over a meal one evening. "I try to propose a settlement that both parties can accept. The goal is to restore balance within the community. Usually a murderer cannot pay the compensation for the one killed, so the burden falls on his kin to do so. So those inclined to violence think twice before the act is performed, as it affects their entire family."

8

THE NEW LAND DIVISION

I RELAX as I think about these affairs and sink into reverie, allowing my mind to be drawn back into the past, back to the time of the establishment of the new land division on the eastern side of the Inland Sea.

After my return from my successful reconnaissance of the Ennu lands beyond the eastern mountains as well as my discovery of horses, I considered at length the protocol of the project that would be involved in capturing, taming, and bringing horses back to the land divisions around the Inland Sea. This had been the foremost objective of my journey inland—to explore the lands east of the mountains in order to find horses. They are herd animals, and as my mind followed the great trek I had made into the Ennu lands, I realized that a road would have to be cut through the great forest and that a new community would have to be established on the eastern side of the Inland Sea to support an ongoing series of satellite communities into the continent's interior.

There was also the issue of the great escarpment east of the lowland forests, the one that ran north and south that I had climbed to gain access to the continent's interior. It was very high, and it ran parallel to the mountains farther to the east, creating a formidable geographic blockade between the lowlands and the plateau above that gave access to the mountains and to the Ennu lands beyond them. How would I get a herd of horses down that barrier, I wondered?

I pause and look at what I have written, then pick up a smaller brush, trim it, and dip it into the ink. This is where things get interesting. I continue to write . . .

One night, in response to a protracted amorous encounter with my lady Maraea, the mystic power occurred, and I was drawn back into relationship with my ancestor. And it was in response to this connection with the American's mind and soul that I learned something of great importance.

I knew that the American had been merged with me, off and on, through my long walk as well as during much of my time with the Ennu peoples. Having been there, my ancestor was also aware of the challenges that the escarpment presented. The American had foreseen this problem with relationship to the bringing of horses back to the lowlands, and in response, he had engaged in a geographic journey of reconnaissance in his own slice of time—a time in which the escarpment did not yet exist.

The American had lived in a large community on the eastern side of the great valley that was inundated by the Inland Sea when the oceans rose, and yet known to him was a large volcano in the mountainous hills that edge the east side of this valley to the north. In the American's time, this volcano was known as Las Sen [Lassen], a strange name, and yet the American reasoned that the great crack in the Earth that ran north and south and gave rise to the escarpment would run directly into what he thought of as a volcanic plug, whatever that is. North of the mountain, he reasoned, the crack might not exist, nor the escarpment, so he had driven his "car" in a great circle route over several days, looking for a way into the interior of the continent north of Las Sen.

And he had found one: a route that followed a river that flowed west out of the uplifted country north of Las Sen, where the mountains were less formidable than in the south. The land there slowly rose—but without the high peaks—and the river wandered ever across the land, originating in a heavily timbered valley in the high country north and east of the volcanic mountain. From this valley, there were two routes into what my ancestor calls the Great Basin—one to the south from the river's source across uplifted but mostly flat lava fields, and one somewhat to the north that cut through a narrow canyon toward a broad valley with a shallow lake that was in the Great Basin in his time.

I learned about the American's reconnaissance through our connection across the Dreaming. Then when

Governor Ruth Kahalopuna, Maraea's grandmother, encouraged me to establish a new land division to the east and find a route into the interior, I had organized a dry-season expedition of several dozen people possessing various skills and abilities. We had sailed north in a large voyaging canoe, locating the volcano Las Sen, as well as the outlet of the large river into the Inland Sea still farther to the north.

Leaving most of my compatriots to establish the beginnings of a *kulanakauhale*—a village—on the high land above the river mouth, I had traveled rapidly with a dozen hunters through the great forests to the east, following the river and marking our passage on the great trees. We had discovered that the American's theory was correct. The land rose toward the uplifted eastern highlands, but the great escarpment was absent north of the volcano. This was confirmation that we had found the route to cut the road through the forest and into the raised uplands, giving us access into the Ennu country, where we could capture horses and tame them.

Much was accomplished during those three lunar cycles during our short dry season. I returned to the capitol before the rains returned and drafted a proposal that allowed me to interface with all the ruling families of the land divisions. It was necessary to acquire the necessary supplies of timber and thatch for housing; shaped stone for walkways, walls, and foundations; drainage ditches to carry off rainwater; and all the implements, tools, and food for the skilled labor to accomplish the project of creating a string of new communities at the river's mouth as well as into the interior. I encouraged all the ruling families to contribute and to convince everyone of the worthiness of this project and how it might enhance life in the growing number of towns and villages around the Inland Sea.

This produced a flow of materials and skilled laborers to create the foundation for the new community at the river mouth. Landsmen and foresters were brought to create cleared fields for agriculture and fencing for livestock. This working community continued to develop, and became self-sufficient within three seasonal cycles. It had then taken an additional two cycles to complete the cutting of the road into the interior, during which time, more ruins of American sitis had been discovered in the forest. They were small in contrast to the great ones to the south.

At times, the river wandered across largely flat areas, and the road building was easy. At others, the river was constrained into rather short, narrow gorges that dropped steeply, so the road was cut across the intervening higher lands to join the river valley again farther to the east.

The charcoal burners had accompanied my teams, burning the toppled trees and creating charcoal that was sent back to all the land divisions. It was a multifaceted project that worked well, and during this time, my exploratory team and I were constantly on the move, scouting the terrain and determining the easiest route. It was on one such evening in the forest that I had another dream connection with my ancestor. It had been many seasonal cycles since the last one, so I was unprepared when it occurred.

I was almost asleep in my hammock slung between the major branches of a large tree in the mountain forest when the physical paralysis hit, filling me with ecstatic feelings of power that soared, and drawing me into a deep trance state in which an awareness awaited me, one I knew well.

"Warm greetings, descendant," came the voice in Old English.

9

THE DREAM

My excitement surged. We were in connection once again, mind to mind, and the thoughtline between us then moved in a strange direction, one that took me by surprise.

The American said, "I am aware of your deep commitment to your lady Maraea. I am also aware that she may be the future embodiment of my lady Jill . . . as you may be of me. It seems that she and I have found each other again in our long journey across eternity." Long pause. The thoughtline then shifted.

"Allow me to confirm my relationship with a Hawaiian kahuna elder during the last years of his life. He passed much of his knowledge to Jill and me. It was his intention, I believe, that I commit this knowledge to memory. He wished for me to pass his knowledge of Polynesian mystical wisdom to you, and he saw our occasional connections as a way that this might be accomplished."

As I came fully awake, my astonishment increased exponentially as another thoughtline began, a long progression of thinking and feeling, of concepts and percepts, all mixed up together and presented to my conscious awareness like the flowing of a river of sensory information. I watched this flow, entranced, until it finally came to a stop. Then, the connection slowly faded, the paralysis that had held me captive slowly eased, and it was over. In my mind, a word from my ancestor floated, the word *transmission*. This word in Old English was not familiar to me.

I stayed awake the rest of the night reviewing all that I had received, organizing it all into a form that made sense to me. And as the light of early dawn glowed in the eastern skies, the first birdcall brought me back to myself. My sense of amazement increased by the moment, accompanied by an immense feeling of joy. This was something quite extraordinary, I knew, but what? I would soon know the answer.

This was the beginning of my reception of the *manao*, the wisdom, of the kahuna Hale Makua—the knowledge that he had wished to convey across the space-time continuum through the American so that it would be transmitted to me and to my society. In this way, his understanding of his culture and the past history of the Polynesian peoples would be preserved to enlighten our current communities here on the American mainland.

10

———

RETURN

PERIODICALLY I RETURNED HOME to the Kahalopuna land division from the ongoing project at the end of our short dry season before the rains began. There, I reported on the team's progress to the old Governor while she was still alive, and to Maraea as well. Both were captivated by the progress that my chosen team and I had made.

These were always intense reunions with my wife at the heart level, infused with our great affection for each other as well as our strong mutual attraction. On one such evening after an extended marital encounter, we lay relaxed in each other's arms, and then I felt the awareness of the American in my mind, so I slowly let the sensual memories of my lady go.

I felt the American's acquiescence, his agreement with a lingering feeling of "belonging to." For the American is also part of this dynamic; how could he not be? Our connections have often happened in response to similar activities, verging on those that are identical, in his life and time and mine. And many have been the episodes in which he has been abed with his wife and me with mine. This has created a sense of shared intimacy that is quite reassuring, as well as more than acceptable. My ancestor's wife is very beautiful, and like my wife here, she possesses that gift of slender physical grace. She is also a Chief like Maraea, with a sparkling sense of humor and an incisive mind that misses nothing. She and my ancestor share a great love, as I do with Maraea. They are much alike.

11

AIKU

I PUT down the brush and slip into meditation as images of the past emerge for consideration, including memories of the great forest. It is a time for sharing this, I think. I glance at the spirit stone, connect with the spirit within it, then return to the sheet of paper on my writing table.

I had traveled through the great lowland forest around the Inland Sea many times in my youth in the company of an elder hunter and kahuna mystic named Nagai. He had taught me well about how to survive and navigate through this wooded world. But he had passed into the company of his ancestors many years ago, so now I was alone on my long walk beyond the mountains and into the Ennu lands. Yet he did come in spirit here and there to offer advice and guidance.

So the forest life was familiar to me, essential knowl-edge in this new time as I surveyed a possible route into the interior. But this time I had a team, and among them was a most interesting young man named Aiku. He is a grandson of Nagai and resembles him in his appearance and also in his mindset. I remember how Nagai's spirit had accompanied me during my long trek, providing insight and guidance. And now his descendant had come into relationship with me quite by accident, *if accidents actually happen*, I think, brush poised above the paper.

The circumstances of our initial meetings were, on the whole, rather inconsequential. Yet somehow, Aiku became part of the team involved in creating the new settlement at the river's mouth and the road into the interior. His contributions to the success of this great endeavor were manifested daily. Aiku seemed to be an inseparable part of the forest. He was a hunter of unsurpassed skill, and his knowledge of the forest was quite extraordinary. He was much like his grandfather in many ways, and he provided guidance and sustenance in the form of food on a daily basis, which kept us all well fed. He was simply naturally adept at it.

I hadn't known that Aiku had his grandfather's mystic ability until one day when we were surveying the route across a highland region around an area where the river that flowed westward cut through a gorge. It wasn't a deep gorge, yet it was definitely a gorge. The team all sat quietly for a midday meal of dried meat and fruit; and Aiku, like all of us, had his woven hammock slung around his waist along with a longish coil of rope. His bow and quiver of arrows were slung across his back, with his game bags for meat hung under his arms on both sides. A rain cape of ti leaves woven into netting and soaked with kukui oil was slung over a shoulder, and his black stone knife in a sheath hung down from his waist belt, as was the case with all of us. A net bag with fire starters and some medicines and an extra pair of sandals hung around his torso, and a long spear with a metal point completed his accoutrements. In the event we encountered tigers or large forest pigs, Aiku was a match for both. He was a free agent, completely in sync with his environment, as was I, having walked this path before. The two of us were in complete alignment.

We got on well from the start, and on this particular day, near the gorge, Aiku had asked me, respectfully, if I had a special feeling for spotted tigers. I paused, and looking into the younger man's eyes, I saw his clairvoyance. I came to a decision and answered that I did.

"I feel that there is one observing us from that hillside, Chief Nainoa." Aiku gestured upward with his bow tip at an upland seen through a break in the trees. "Perhaps it is interested in you." Aiku let the conversation drift.

I scanned the younger man again and then told him the story—a rather long one—about my relationship with this spirit helper . . . and my ancestor's connection with it as well. (The American has written about this in his books.)

Aiku listened intently and then responded. "As we come into the awareness of the minds that live in our forests, we understand that each of them is an expression of a singular mind—a mind sourced into them by the spirit of the animal or plant or tree of which each is an expression. We discover that each being, or thing possesses its own personal spiritual aspect or force, and that each may be very much aware of us, as well as who and what we are."

He thought for a moment, then observed: "Then there are the Forest Lords; they perceive us as High Beings because of the creative capacities of our minded selves. They know what we can do but only rarely reveal themselves to us. They have their own agendas."

Aiku paused as a crow alighted in the tree branch above him. The crow observed him dispassionately and waited. Aiku watched the crow in return. Then he offered the crow a morsel of his meal, which the crow accepted. "You see?" he said, turning to me. "I suspect, too, that when one crow knows something, they all know it. They have a group mind to which all crows may have access. Now that I have fed this one, we may expect more crows to find us." And they did.

Throughout our conversation, Aiku watched me with focused attention. "And what of those Higher Beings above us in the Upper Realms of spirit, Chief Nainoa?" Aiku asked with a shy smile. "There are those spiritual oversouls who source us into existence, into new bodies for each life, and there are those who are their teachers and *kahus* [keepers] who maintain an active interest in us, their students' embodiments. Even so, they rarely intrude or influence us in any way." The younger man observed me closely and added, "Yet they are always with us, always aware of every thought we think, every emotion we feel, every experience we engage in, every action we take, and they support us in who and what we are becoming."

I pause in my writing again and consider my affection for this young man. Aiku's insights about the Higher Intelligences caught me off guard on that day, yet in retrospect, his thoughts were much in alignment with what I now know to be true. I consider the younger man's perceptions at some length, then continue to write.

I became aware that this young man possesses Nagai's spiritual power, his *ike*. Maybe he is Nagai, back for another round in the physical world. I believe that Aiku was born after Nagai's passing, but I will have to ask him to be sure. This was the beginning of our relationship, and with it, I felt the presence of my old friend and mentor slip quietly back into my life. From that day on, Aiku stayed close, occasionally expressing a thought, an opinion, or an observation; and I came to value his perceptiveness and insight, older man to younger man. He anticipated what needed to be done, and he did it.

Our reconnaissance continued throughout that dry season and extended through the dry seasons of the next three cycles, creating the route for the great road to be cut into the interior. In response to my ancestors' insights, it was also decided that we would create satellite communities along the new road one day's travel from each other. And at the end of the road through the mountains, another larger community would take form near or in the Ennu lands. Our explorations provided valuable information, and with the return of the rains each year, we all withdrew to our land divisions, and I returned to the capitol.

I was in Aiku's company as I scouted the long route into the interior that would become our road. We located the source of the river as well as the fairly level forested upland valley from which it originates. We also managed to scout out two possible routes into the Ennu lands, one to the north and one to the south. As I gazed across those hazy regions with their wooded grasslands and rangy lakes once again, Aiku asked me about the behavior of horses, but I had begun thinking about Kenojelak. It had been a long time.

12

____

KENOJELAK

SINCE THAT TIME, many such connections have occurred between the American and me, and in one of them, my ancestor told me that his readership constantly asks him about Kenojelak, my Ennu wife. She apparently made quite an impression through his writings about my time with her. And how could she not? She is a beautiful, strong, passionate woman, very free spirited, and she answers to no one but herself.

We had enjoyed a yearlong engagement during the time I lived with the Ennu; and when I returned to the Hawaiian settlements, Kenojelak remained with her people. She is a mystic, like myself, and at that time she had been informed by the spiritual forces with whom she is in relationship that she would be _ungagok_, a shaman and medicine woman for her people. And she has become just that . . . but this is getting ahead of the story I need to tell.

When we finally met again, many years had passed, and it was during this period that I married my lady Maraea. This was also the time in which I had designed the project to acquire horses from the interior and set it into motion. In the beginning, because of the relatively short dry seasons, the large crew of people involved in the project (as I came to think of it) could only devote themselves to it for perhaps three or four lunar cycles before the rains returned and the lowlands around the Inland Sea became swamplands, inundated for the rest of the year.

Once the core of the new community was in place at the river's mouth, with living quarters built and fields cleared and planted for food, those who would live and work there in the years to come remained, and the project's forward momentum was maintained.

When the road into the interior is finally completed, the choice of where and how to capture horses might be planned according to my ancestor's directions. But for now, a large sector of the grassy land near a lake has been chosen because the water will provide for the horses, and the dampness of the ground around the lake's edge will maintain fresh grasses for forage all year long. The project is in process and now involves enclosing this quadrant of land and part of the lake with a high split-rail fence. This is proving to be very time-consuming, and a large satellite community has been created at some distance in the high valley at the river's source to house and feed the workers, hunters, and stockpeople and their families.

In the year that has just passed, I visited and inspected

the work accomplished so far. Trees were being felled and split into long rails, with a large crew devoted to creating and erecting this fence. My ancestor calls it a *corral*, an interesting word from the past. After offering my insights and directives as to what needed to be done and how, there was little else for me to do; and with several lunar cycles at my disposal, I decided to see if I could track down William's people once again and visit with Kenojelak.

We had made contact with several Ennu bands over the years when we arrived at the Basin. And although I had not met these Ennu before, they had heard about me . . . the tall foreigner from the west named Nainoapak, the suffix *–pak* referring to my great height. And indeed, the Ennu are considerably shorter than most of us Hawaiians. Our meetings with them were exciting for all of us, and since I can speak the Ennu language, they were also cordial and infused with *aloha*. We hunted and feasted together, and generally enjoyed their company until they departed and moved north.

They knew of William and his band to the south. Their hunting lands extended to the north and east, however, so they had never met them. I wondered if Kenojelak would eventually hear through word of mouth that I was back in her country once again. I guessed that she and her band might be living below that scarred mountain in their dry-season camp and estimated that it would take at least five days to get there, maybe more. So, I elected to take Aiku with me.

It was the season of migrating birds, and we set out early one morning, following the waterfowl southward. We crossed the highland area until it descended into the edge of a large lake that sent a long finger toward the mountains to the west. There did not appear to be any crocodiles in these wetlands, so we feasted on fish obtained from the lake almost daily.

We followed the edge of the Basin ever southward, keeping the mountains to our right and the sporadic lakes and marshes to our left. At night, we retreated to the forest margin to escape the mosquitos, and we slept high in the trees in our hammocks, as we sometimes heard the big cats that my ancestor calls *lions* roaring in the darkness. Fortunately, they were at some distance, and we did not encounter any, nor any of the striped tigers, although we saw their scat.

During the days, the game was also plentiful; and we hunted, paused to dress out the meat, and ate well. I pointed out several herds of the long-horned cattle from whom we kept our distance, and we saw several large herds of horses that kept their distance from us. At one river crossing, we encountered a small herd of those fantastic creatures my ancestor calls *elephants*. We have forest elephants to the west, but these seemed to be a different type, with larger ears. When they detected us, they withdrew with their strange vocalizations.

Aiku and I traveled together in silence for much of the time, yet we enjoyed telling stories of our lives around the fire at night, and we got to know one another very well. I continued to wonder if he was Nagai the hunter, returned for another life to explore with me once again. The resemblance was striking.

We finally arrived at the vast ruined city that my ancestor told me was once called *Reno*. With the collapse of the American civilization, it had been abandoned and was now covered in woodlands and grasses. Yet in many places, the stone foundations of buildings and chimneys projected upward, with the largest stone ruins emerging from earthen mounds in the center.

A small river ran through the site that Aiku and I crossed at a shallow ford. We bathed and then ran down and hooked several large fish with our unstrung bows, tossing them up on the bank where we built a fire and feasted. Aiku told me that evening that he was aware that many ghosts inhabited this place and that they were curious about us. He thought they might be the spirits of the people who had once lived there and that they were unhappy ghosts, so we kept the fire built high to negate our unease. We decided to move on the next day, and as we headed south, we kept an eye out for objects of interest as we traversed this haunted place.

We had entered territory that was familiar to me then, and my excitement was rising. We passed the place with steam coming out of the ground, and on the seventh day, by midmorning, there was the valley before us with its lake in the center and the massive scarred mountain to the west. On a high area some distance from the lake, I saw the smoke from campfires, and I knew I had been correct in guessing where William and his band would be.

Upon our final approach, the Ennu dogs spotted us and rushed down the slope to confront us. I saw several I had known in the past and remembered their names— and they remembered me after all these years. Within moments, these fierce guardians became friendly. They escorted us to the camp where the entire community was lined up, observing us in silence.

Then William recognized me. He ran to me and wrapped me in his strong arms as we rubbed our noses and faces together. He laughed with joy, exclaiming "Heeeeee!" again and again; and I heard my name being spoken, passing from mouth to mouth as the volume grew. I looked for Kenojelak but didn't see her. William saw my searching look and said knowingly, "She is at the stream with the other women, bathing and drawing water for the camp." He grinned with the delight of it. Kenojelak was his daughter.

We spent much of the afternoon in conference, with me introducing Aiku and describing our relationship, as well as the nature of the project itself. The whole issue of capturing and breeding horses was totally foreign to the Ennu. They were hunter-gatherers, and from their perspective, horses were good to eat. Why would anyone want to possess them?

I shared much of what had transpired since we parted company so many years ago, including my elevation in status within my communities. This meant nothing to the

Ennu, who had an egalitarian society. They didn't understand it or see why it was important, but everyone smiled and nodded as though they did. I also described my marriage to Maraea and the birth of our two children, to which everyone reacted with delight. Ennu society was quite fluid in terms of primary relationships; many women had co-husbands, and many men had co-wives. In addition, many migrated from marriage to marriage, with serial mates across time. This was the norm among them.

William conveyed much information to me as well as with the band sitting around us listening raptly. I learned who had passed, who had been born, and who had left the band for parts unknown, often marrying out. William's wife, Kalvak, had died, and her bones were tied in a tree out on the plain somewhere. William looked much the same, yet his hair and frizzy beard were now quite white, giving him the appearance of a High Medicine Man, which in fact he was. I noted that some of the young Ennu girls still in camp were looking at Aiku with frank appraisal. He was going to have an interesting visit.

I translated our conversations for Aiku as the afternoon progressed, and he listened with interest. I saw his gaze scanning the Ennu camp, taking in details. I have mentioned before how simple their houses are, looking more like round brushy tents made of samplings with leaves and grasses woven in. Aiku had never before seen people like this or heard an alien language. Then there was their clothing and housing, and I could tell that he was fascinated. The men wore a kind of breech-clout that passed between the legs and was pulled upward front and back and tied with cords around the waist, then were allowed to drop, forming a kind of apron that fell to the knees, front and back. When the women returned, he would see that they were dressed much the same, with longer aprons. Both men and women were bare above the waist.

We were given water to drink and shards of dried and smoked meat to eat while we talked. I remembered the taste of the meat so well. As we chewed with gusto, Aiku raised his eyebrows at me. "Horse," I replied. "Good, isn't it?" The stories went on, and I knew that they would continue to be told every day and every evening as long as we stayed with the Ennu, to be repeated and retold for years, even perhaps for generations, after we departed.

The women arrived back before the twilight. As they emerged from the riverine forest that bracketed the stream in the distance, I watched them and looked for a slender woman taller than the rest. And there she was. I stood and saw the flash of her smile in the distance. The women were carrying large bladders of some animal filled with water. On final approach, she handed her burdens to another, including the carrying basket slung across her back, and took me into her arms without speaking, rubbing her nose and face against mine before kissing me with fervor. She laughed with the delight of it as her breasts rubbed against my chest. I remembered that laugh, and I remembered her wonderful scent. The Ennu around us cheered and burst into a song. As we continued to embrace, I heard my name and hers woven into the song.

Then I saw the girl. She was with Kenojelak and was observing me solemnly. She was perhaps eight or nine years old, skinny as a stick and taller that the other children I could see. She had long tangled hair and big blue eyes like her father. Kenojelak drew her into our embrace, and I squatted down to rub noses. She did so shyly, looking at me with wonder. Kenojelak spoke to her. "This is your father." Then to me: "Her name is Kalvak; we named her after her grandmother."

I grinned at her. "Kalvak," I said, and gathered her into my arms for a big hug. She hugged me back, then withdrew shyly behind her mother.

That evening lasted for many hours, with many stories being told around the central fire over the evening meal, mostly meat with some cattail roots from the lake. Little Kalvak was falling asleep when she finally allowed herself to be drawn into one of the shelters by an older woman I remembered, and Aiku allowed himself to be drawn by William into his shelter, the two speaking in gesture. And then the community withdrew, and it was just Kenojelak and me, alone.

I saw myself through her eyes and realized that I had aged and put on some weight in response to my more sedentary lifestyle in the capitol. Yet I still looked fit, and my body was muscular, my blue eyes offset by the mahogany of my skin tone, with my high cheekbones and broad nose accentuating my bearded jawline. A series of tattoos descended the left side of my face from my hair-line to my beard, and my open cloak revealed that they continued down that side of my body, culminating at my left ankle—long lines of triangles, circles, and nested curves. They expressed a story on the one hand and revealed my membership in the Order of Kahuna on the other. My thick black hair, now with traces of gray at the temples, shone with health, pulled back into a long pony-tail draped over one shoulder and falling almost to my waist.

And Kenojelak? There were traces of gray in her dark hair as well, and new lines around her eyes and mouth. She was lean, as were all the Ennu; and her long, slender legs guaranteed that she was the tallest member of her band. Her lovely face and eyes were framed by her thick braids; and her muscular body, mostly revealed by her minimal clothing, was beautiful. In observing her fully, I felt my blood sparkling with light.

For a long period, we simply stared into each other's eyes across the fire, and it was as if information was being passed between us mentally and emotionally. The feelings we held for each other were reignited once again. We spoke of this or that, small things, as a way of reconnect-ing. I learned that she had not taken another mate since my departure years ago, and that she was an *ungagok*, or spiritwalker, for her people, what my ancestor calls a *shaman*. She had become an accomplished healer, and her talents were in constant demand by other Ennu bands out there on the wooded grasslands.

I told her about my relationships with Maraea and the children we had created, and she smiled. "I knew you would do this, Nainoapak. You have become a Big Man. My father, William, is proud to call you son. And I know you . . . and who you are."

As the fire died down, she stood and took me by the hand, drawing me into her shelter. Our reunion was intense and protracted, lasting most of the night. I was aware that our dance had two expressions—the dance of our bodies and the dance of our hearts. It was a beautiful thing, body to body, soul to soul, and I realized how much I had missed this wonderful woman. In the wee hours, holding her in my arms and savoring her scent, I reflected on my relationships with Maraea and now once again with Kenojelak, and I saw the structure of my life blended with these two powerful women as part of my foundation. Then a memory came up in my mind, one that was not my own.

I saw an image of my ancestor walking with three tribal men out in the deserts of Africa. They all looked up into the vastness of the blue sky and saw an eagle. After a thoughtful pause, one of the men looking at the bird said, "What a gift is this life. We must always honor the gift. Otherwise it might just fly away."

This memory faded, and I was aware that my ancestor was in residence. I looked at my lover and Ennu wife in the dim light. We were both stretched out naked on her furs and were lying in each other's arms. We were honoring the gift of this moment.

Of course, we had to endure much good-natured teasing and sexual innuendos from the community in the days to come, and Kenojelak gave back as good as she got. The mood was definitely elevated as the sun rose that morning, and the endless flow of stories and songs that had begun the previous evening took form once again.

I watched Kenojelak at all times; I could not take my eyes off her, and this did not escape the notice of the assemblage of people around us, inspiring more jokes and sometimes outright vulgar observations. I translated some of the Ennu comments for Aiku, and he blushed. Little Kalvak watched me all the time too, and I had the sense that she had her mother's visionary ability and could see into the core of my soul.

13

ENNU LIFE

I KNEW that we had two months of time, maybe three, before we had to return to our land divisions around the Inland Sea for the long rains. And we made the best of it. Aiku attracted the attentions of an Ennu girl, and a new shelter was made for them. We hunted with the men, and Aiku got his first close look at horses. And as we hunted, it was always in my mind that we would try to capture a herd and domesticate them once the new settlement was established on the edge of the Great Basin. Accordingly, I studied the horses as well as their "horse society" as closely as I could. The Ennu also told me much.

I made friends with little Kalvak and spent a great deal of time with her and her mother. Kenojelak and I took up the habit of bathing together in private once again, and as often as not, this led to a joyous celebration of the senses. She told me stories of her life in the band during the years of our separation. These included details of the healing rituals she had created and performed with the help of her spirits, as well as the back-end stories of each encounter. She sang me songs; teased me unmercifully; and made mad, passionate love with me as often as possible. We were a very happy couple!

Yet our passion always had a tinge of sadness to it, as we both knew that our time together would come to an end – at least for this year. But I also knew that my responsibilities to my project would bring me back to the Ennu lands every dry season from then on, and I assured her of continued visits in the years to come.

When William's band migrated out into their hunting grounds during our time with them, Aiku and I went with them. My relationship with Kenojelak's father was as warm as ever, and William and I spent long evenings under the starry sky talking about everything from cosmology to the amusing details of everyday life. William was getting old, and his mind would frequently wander down trails from the past, providing me with a rich supply of lore about the Ennu people and their culture. As often as not, Aiku was the third member of our discussions, and I translated the old hunter's words for him as best I could.

The members of William's band took a shine to Aiku, and they gave him lessons in the Ennu language at every opportunity. Slowly, he began to understand what was being said, and his attempts at responding were met with hilarity before the Ennu corrected him in his efforts to talk the talk.

When another band camped with us over several weeks, Kenojelak's healing skills were in high demand; and she and I frequently worked together, empowering the sufferer, correctly diagnosing the problem through trance, extracting the illness causing intrusions, and restoring the fabric of the sufferer's soul. As she and I complemented each other's abilities and visionary perceptions, these were rich experiences, and my prestige among the Ennu was considerably enhanced. Quite suddenly, the word *ungagok* was being applied to *me*.

In one of these healings, something interesting happened. A young woman from the other band had an affliction in which every time she had her monthlies, she would suffer great pain. Her family prevailed upon Kenojelak to heal her, and she drew me into the dynamic. Virtually everyone in both bands turned up for the ceremony, perhaps more than 50 Ennu.

The woman lay down on a bed of furs in the shade of some overarching trees near the big lake, and William drummed for us. Kenojelak lay down on one side of the woman, with me on the other. As we settled into the visionary state in response to the drum, I allowed my mind to turn toward the woman. As my vision came up, I clearly perceived something dark in her lower belly. I sat up and saw that Kenojelak was also sitting up and staring into the woman's stomach area and making flowing gestures over her torso.

At this point, another ungagok from the other band joined William with his drum, and they began to drum together, drawing on the life force and setting up a powerful field of *mana* [spiritual energy] around the three of us. Kenojelak looked at me and pointed at the girl's belly. Bringing my face down near to her body, I looked closer as the trance state gripped me in its invisible fist. Just above the edge of her leather apron, the darkness within was revealed to be a spider clamped around the woman's womb.

I glanced up at Kenojelak, who made a gesture that indicated I should take it out. So, I sat up and focused, and called on one of my spirits, a water bird with a long bill. Almost immediately, a night heron appeared, the long black feather down its back and its bright red eyes regarding me with interest. It perched on my arm. Allow me to say that this was not a physical bird; it was a spirit bird that sometimes worked with me to remove internal intrusive elements from individuals' bodies. In the same way, the intrusion wasn't a physical spider. It was just the way I happened to see it.

Using nonverbal communication, I asked the bird to observe the spider, which it did. Then I asked it to remove the offending intrusion with no parts left behind. After a moment's consideration of my request, the bird hopped down on the girl's belly, and she winced as she felt the energy flow. Kenojelak was singing a healing song and making gestures over the woman; and I watched, intrigued, as the bird slid its bill into the woman and gently gripped the spider, removing it in its entirety in one smooth movement. The woman sighed . . . and the bird ate the spider.

Kenojelak then opened her mind and did divination work to ascertain the source of the intrusion. As it turned out, another young woman in the band was jealous of this girl, and her negative thoughts had generated the intrusive element that she had then directed at the sufferer with the intent to do harm. This is what my ancestor calls an example of *negative witchcraft*.

So Kenojelak and several women from both bands performed a powerful cleansing ceremony for the offender, bringing her to realize and accept what she had done and reestablishing harmony between the two women and balance within the band. I would learn in years to come that my ancestor used a similar ceremony in a similar way to be of service to a young woman in *his* time, and interestingly, that ceremony occurred in a community in what he called Northern California, near where we are establishing a new settlement. That is amazing, I think.

That evening, in the lazy aftermath of lovemaking, Kenojelak told me more stories about her life, and I shared more stories about mine. In this way, we came to include each other in our separate lives, and I knew I would love her forever.

I lay awake, listening to her breathing, feeling my great affection for her; and then a sense of warmth washed up my body, the blood in my ears started to hiss, and in moments the exquisite pressure took me into its invisible fist. As my body became paralyzed, the great grid of light lines appeared, and the sense of movement outward became primary. I found myself racing along a light line toward that curious crescent of light that appeared to be opening. As I braced for the impact, I shot through . . . and then I was there.

14

THE MEETING

As my vision came up, I found myself standing under a small grove of trees with large shiny leaves, some of which were dark green, some red. I could hear the sound of waves. I was in the center of a circle, an area of black sand surrounded by a perimeter of large ocean-tumbled beach stones of black lava that were arranged to form a long, continuous stone "bench" that wrapped around the central area. To one side, a stand of tall palms formed a cluster, beyond which the massive black stonewall of a big heiau temple platform was just visible through more trees. Behind me stretched a wide bay of sparkling water with the blue ocean beyond, and to my left, the tall escarpment of a monumental cliff could be clearly seen. I was merged with the American.

I glanced beyond and saw the house with its tall thatch roof and broad lanai above what appeared to be a freshwater pond. Beyond it was a thick stand of trees, including a tamarind fruit with countless dusty-gray brown pods . . . and looking further, I saw the slope of a huge mountain reaching up toward the sky. It was my ancestor's "sacred garden," his personal place of power and healing in the dreamtime. There was a woman watching from the lanai. I had met her before and remembered that her name was Tehura. I turned my attention to the American and I thought; *This is so real . . .*

"Yes, it is," the American replied to my thought in Old English. "It is the nature of the dream field to reshape itself in response to the dreamers . . . and that is us in this case. On this occasion, we are going to meet someone of singular importance to us both." The American fell silent, and we allowed our dreaming selves to settle onto a stone seat beneath the trees. From the American's mind, I knew that these were kamani trees. The stones were water smooth and cool. The American assumed a relaxed repose in the dappled shade of the trees, with the blue ocean of Kealakekua Bay beyond black lava stones that backed the small beach.

I watched the American with interest. His first name, Hank, was a variant of his true name, Henry. He had put on some weight as well, and his hair was now streaked with gray—especially his beard. In bare feet and dressed in a black shirt and pale brown pants, he seemed totally at ease in this locality, as he should have, for it was his place in the Middle Worlds of Dream. We had met here before, which the American has written about in the past, but the circle of stone seats under the kamani trees, with the cleared circular area of black sand in the center, had not been present then. Someone had created it in the interim. The American smiled again and addressed me.

"Chief Nainoa . . ." He paused and bowed, greeting me with respect. I grinned, rose, and made a dignified bow in return, then sat again. I was wonderstruck at the vividness of this visionary encounter. Then I spoke.

"Esteemed ancestor, you and I have an extraordinary connection. The reason, the meaning of our trail crossings, the *why* of them, has become increasingly clear to me in my years of meditation and reflection. I have become aware that you and I have a singular shape to the work that we have signed up for as we advance in our soul age across time. I have come to believe that you and I were destined to create a timeline between us, so that if your civilization is headed toward collapse—and you have indicated that this seems to be the case—my future time will already exist, allowing the souls embodied in your time to relocate into mine. What comes in between, I do not know, for the only sources of information I have are your mind and my own."

There was silence in our conjoined awarenesses as these thoughts were considered. The American responded: "It's true. We've been working with Time, and it occurs to me that you and I are in the process of becoming *Weavers of Time*." He paused in deep thought. "Whatever that means . . ." A longer pause ensued. "As you may know, there are advanced souls among the Higher Organizing Intelligences in the Upper Levels of the spirit worlds who work with Time. And they have very specific jobs at certain localities in the subtle realms with relation to the reincarnational cycle here on planet Earth.

"There is the locality in the Upper Worlds in what I call the Planning and Re-entry Center, where we are given glimpses of the future lives available to us before we reincarnate. That is also the place where we make the choice for that life. The center appears to be under the control of advanced souls called the Time Masters. It is they who weave Time into the time lines. Perhaps you and I are Time Masters-in-training."

We considered this in silence. Then the American closed his eyes, and through our soul connection, I knew that he was focused and extending an invitation . . . but to whom? Then he opened his eyes and gestured to one side. In the center of the cleared area of stacked black beach stones appeared a luminous form—a tall, vertical column of undulating, misty-blue light that resolved itself into a large blue sphere. As we watched breathlessly, the sphere abruptly elongated into an image of a being made of light, a tall human at least twice our height who stepped forward. It was a woman, and she had long flowing hair and many layers of voluminous blue coverings all the way to her feet. Her large gray eyes looked down upon us both. She looked serious, as if she meant business.

In my mind a name appeared. I did not know where this name came from, or who this spiritual personage might be, but the image of this statuesque woman in my mind's eye held me captive – immobile. Then she smiled, and it was as though the sun had come out.

In my peripheral vision, I saw the American bow toward the monumental woman, who bowed in return . . . and then he spoke to me in Old English. "This great being is our Spirit Guide. She is the teacher and the caretaker of our immortal Oversoul, our shared Aumakua." The American glanced at the tall luminous being and added, "She has come to make your acquaintance, as she may be a pivotal player in whatever comes next."

A warm voice then appeared in my mind, speaking in perfect Hawaiian, as it was once known in the home islands. "*Aloha pumehana, Ali'i Nainoa Kaneohe. 'E 'ola mau loa. 'Eli 'eli kau mai* . . . a warmhearted aloha to you, Chief Nainoa. Long life and may a profound reverence alight on you."

Then she turned to the American, who bowed his head in deference. Her voice in Old English appeared in my mind: "You and your descendant do indeed make a magnificent pair. You have a great destiny that stretches before you. How wonderful that it has finally come to pass after so many millennia."

She paused and turned to me, again continuing in Hawaiian. "I have been privileged to be part of the spiritual unfolding of your shared Aumakua since it came into being as a soul. This reveals that you, both of you and your shared Spirit Soul, were assigned to me at your Oversoul's beginning. I have been your Oversoul's caretaker for a very long time . . . across countless embodiments. I will be with you forever as your teacher and your spirit friend.

"Those of us among the Higher Organizing Intelligences who are involved in mentoring souls having the human experience usually do not get involved in the lives of the embodied beings sourced into that life by an Oversoul. But occasionally, as is the case in this moment, it seems appropriate."

She paused, then realizing that the American did not understand, she switched to Old English, and her voice continued.

"Everyone has a personal spirit guide. They are protectors and teachers." She paused again and glanced at the American, who joined the conversation.

He said, "Guides are figures of grace because they are part of the fulfillment of our personal and collective destiny. They are complex entities, especially if they are master guides. As such, they often have a junior guide in training, and so some of us have more than one guide. The guides serve as teachers and advisers who may inject ideas into our minds or comfort us as children, leading us through the perils and pains of childhood as imaginary friends. They listen to our prayers and monitor us throughout our lives.

"Sometimes we pick them up as a presence. Sometimes we visualize a face or a figure or hear a voice. Sometimes we simply see a flash of colored light, and this is usually a sign that our guide wishes to communicate with us. All guides have compassion for their students, but teaching approaches vary. Some constantly help souls on Earth, especially those of younger soul age. Others insist that we work on our lessons with little or no help from them, especially the advancing souls.

"Guides are not easy on us, but they aren't judgmental. We are accepted by our guides for who we are. They build morale and instill confidence in us. They motivate us and help us find our courage. They have all passed through their own incarnational embodiments as humans, and they have been through all that we are going through."

He paused and received a warm smile from the spirit woman. I noted that she had now assumed a stature equal to ours, and we were now the same height, eye to eye. She said, "Guides often appear to people who are very religious as figures in their faith—a Christian seeing Jesus, a Jew meeting Moses, or a Muslim meeting the prophet Mohammed. We do this because we know that humans will be more likely to come into relationship with us if we appear to them in a familiar form. I, for example, have chosen to appear on this day as Athena, the Greek goddess of wisdom, in keeping with your ancestor's love of the Classical Period in Ancient Greece.

"And here is something useful to know: Humans can draw on their guides at any time during life on Earth, as their guides are always in connection with them—always. We remain in connection with our charges over thousands of years to assist them in their lessons and trials during countless lives.

"Allow me to add a cautionary note. When our students avoid real problem solving, the guides may make themselves scarce. We cannot assist our charges until they are ready to make changes in their lives so that they can take full advantage of their life's opportunities."

The American said, "A friend of mine has noted that 'our soul's path is unending, as each soul, humanity, and the greater Universe seeks elevation. Soul energy is a light frequency, and from our first incarnation, our divine light frequency called soul initiates a profound climb to higher wisdom. Each soul is also created with the ability to enhance life.'"

Athena responded, "Well said. I am a guide from the angelic realm, from those among us dedicated to being of service to humanity. When I work with embodied souls, we learn together. When embodied souls learn to problem-solve on Earth, I also gain the same awareness. We function as a team. We have access to every thought that you think, every word that you speak, every relationship in which you engage, and every action you take." She paused, then smiled. "This reveals that privacy is truly an illusion – but we try not to intrude."

I sensed that our meeting was coming to an end. Our guide picked up on my thoughts and smiled again. "I will look in on you both from time to time, and yes, I foresee great things for you. Then she turned to me and said, *"A hui hou"* [Until we meet again].

She transformed quickly through the blue sphere and the undulating column of blue light; then she was gone. I glanced at my ancestor, who simply grinned and said, "Welcome to the club. No dues, no committee meetings . . . just reverence."

But he was wrong about the committee meetings.

There was silence in our conjoined minds, and then the American offered these words: "An elder from the Cherokee Nation recently observed, 'Your medicine that you carry is your life, and your life is represented by all those things that you have said, that have been given to you, and that you have given to others. It is all you are and all you have done. Your medicine that you carry is all the things that you bundle together in the form of that which you hold sacred. This is your gift to your world.'"

15

THE RETURN

I EMERGED from the deep trance and lay still in the darkness, considering and wondering all that transpired during this trail crossing on the mystic road. I had been brought into relationship with energies I did not fully understand, yet they had been benevolent. I sensed that my visions were about to change.

I slept then, awakening in the darkness before the dawn to engage in the intense dance of love with Kenoje-lak. Afterward, I held her in my arms and cherished her. My thoughts turned toward the dry season—it was advancing, and soon it would be time to return to the project. Aiku and I would continue to hunt and fish with the Ennu until then, and we would have more philosophical discussions with William. Aiku's command of the Ennu language was coming along. That day and the next, I carved a set of wooden animals for little Kalvak, as well as a doll. Aiku was in love with his new lady, and I knew that our upcoming departure would bring sadness for all of us.

One evening, William spoke about what it means to be ungagok, or as he sometimes said, a *spiritwalker*. Much of what he had to say was known to me, and I knew he was actually directing his thoughts toward Aiku, because he saw that the young man had spirit vision. I translated as best I could. Kenojelak joined us that evening. Here is what I remember, written in the Old English language of my ancestor's time:

"To be an ungagok is a calling," William began. "Those who become spiritually powerful are usually chosen by the spirits, who approach the spiritwalker-to-be in some form or other. Nainoapak told me of his invitation that took place in a ruined siti in the great forest. He was approached by the dark one, and this spirit showed him the existence of the power that we call the *Mystery*. The dark one is the guardian of that realm of power, and if the person descends into fear, then they are not ready, and the entrance remains closed. But for people like ourselves, awe possesses us, and we are drawn in.

"Sometimes the spirits take a very active role in the calling, seizing a person's mind so that they seem to be crazy. Such people often wander, lost in their visions for a while before recovering. Others simply stumble into the tradition because they have the ability to go into trance very easily.

"However the calling happens, spiritwalkers learn to enter the Spirit Worlds more and more deeply, and as they do, they discover that these dreamlike levels of reality are inhabited. They are populated by spirits, some of whom are willing to enter into relationship. And the ungagok, working with these spirit allies, can then do various things, initially for themselves and then increasingly for the members of their band—things like healing, empowerment, hunting magic, and guiding the souls of the dead to where they are supposed to go in the afterlife. Often the spirits impart knowledge to the spiritwalker, such as when Kenojelak was able to learn the source of the problem with that young woman.

"The first stage in becoming a spiritwalker is acquiring the power of spirit vision. Most already have this ability to some degree. The goal is simply to catch glimpses of the spirits and the places in the inner worlds where they live. The second stage involves deepening the visionary ability into an ongoing practice, and it is useful to work with an accomplished older spiritwalker who will introduce the newcomer into the tradition. The elder ungagoks, being closer to the spirit world as their life moves toward its end, often reach a level where they can see the spirits all the time." He sighed wistfully. "My grandmother had this ability.

"The accomplished seeker of visions has the ability to use their own body and mind to create a path between this world of form and the other worlds of spirit. And when the path is open, it allows the healing gifts from the spirits to flow along that path and into our world."

William paused as if considering what to say next.

"The ungagok is the link between the people and the powers of nature; and part of their practice is to maintain a healthy balance in this relationship, creating harmony, good hunting, and abundance. Unless we are respectful of the spirits of the animals we wish to eat, the hunt will not be successful, and the people will be hungry. As you know, we do a ceremony before and after each hunt to maintain this balance." He thought for a minute. "Everyone has their own way of doing ceremony, so I do not think it matters much what you do. What matters is *that* you *do it*. It is about *respect*."

[This is the end of this chapter . . . but not the end of this story. Please read the Postscript and the Editor's Note on the next pages.]

POSTSCRIPT

The purpose of the SharedWisdom programs, books, and healing sessions has been to open people's heart to action. The final chapter of *Timeweaver* was not intended to be the last, given the author anticipated future connections and channeling with Nainoa. Yet it was the last channeled information and can be experienced as an end of the story. Yet…

In keeping with the SharedWisdom purpose and Hank's explicit wishes (see Editor's Note), it is suggested that readers create an ending for themselves, should they feel called to do so. Once created, share it with someone who would appreciate hearing it or reading it – from your open heart now in action and contributing to the opening of others' hearts.

Blessings.

- Jill Kuykendall, December, 2022

EDITOR'S NOTE

I first met Hank Wesselman in 1998, after sending him a "fan email." At the time, I was the Editorial Director for a publishing company in the San Diego area specializing in self-help/mind-body-spirit books, audios, and other products. I had just finished reading *Spiritwalker* and *Medicinemaker*—the first two works in Hank's Spiritwalker series —and I was mesmerized by them.

My email to Hank expressed my admiration for his writing, and he wrote me back, thanking me and informing me that he would soon be conducting a week-long shamanic seminar at Esalen, a retreat community in the lovely coastal town of Big Sur, California. He suggested that I attend. I figured that doing so would serve as both a vacation and an uplifting spiritual experience, so I reserved a spot.

During that magical week, Hank and I developed a friendship that would last until his passing. Several years after the Esalen workshop, I attended another shamanic seminar with Hank and his wife, Jill Kuykendall, in Hawaii, and I also saw Hank over the years when he was in San Diego giving lectures.

In 1999 or so, Hank sent me the manuscript for *Visionseeker*, the third book in the Spiritwalker series; and given my avid enthusiasm for his writings, he asked me if the company where I worked might be interested in publishing this new work. I replied with a resounding *"Yes!"* and *Visionseeker* was published in 2001.

Over the years, Hank and Jill settled permanently in Hawaii, Hank wrote a number of other books (one co-authored with Jill), and he continued giving lectures and conferences throughout the world, in addition to attending to his academic responsibilities.

In February of 2021, with his beloved wife, Jill, by his side, Hank passed away at the age of 79 after a short illness, and people throughout the world mourned his passing. In July of 2022, Jill contacted me and said that she was in possession of Hank's unfinished manuscript for *Timeweaver*, the fourth book in the Spiritwalker series. She asked if I would copyedit it, and asked if the fact that it was unfinished presented a challenge as far as publishing it was concerned. I figured I would think about that issue when I got to the end of the last completed chapter.

The day after I started copyediting, I happened to be talking to my good friend, spiritual medium Marilyn Kapp, the author of *Love Is Greater Than Pain*. I mentioned that I was working on Hank's book, and as we were speaking on the phone, she said that Hank was "coming through in spirit."

With Marilyn as the spiritual channel, the three of us had a delightful and enlightening "conversation," in which Hank imparted many words of wisdom, hope, healing, and love for both his wife, Jill, and their daughters, and for the world at large. He also said that he had an idea for the end of *Timeweaver*. His advice was to have his readers come up with their own endings, and then share those writings with others. Both Marilyn and I thought this was a brilliant solution. When I emailed Jill and told her what had transpired, she was very moved and said that she thought it was a wonderful idea too.

So . . . readers and fans of Hank Wesselman . . . *this is your chance* to tap into Universal Wisdom and come up with your own conclusion to *Timeweaver*. (I was about to say "final manuscript," but you never know what Hank might come up with on the Other Side). Just know that there is no right or wrong way to write what you wish to express. Whatever comes to you will be exactly as it should be.

So, happy reading and writing . . . from Hank's "biggest fan" to all his other "biggest fans." I know that there are a lot of us out there!

- Jill Kramer, July 2022

ACKNOWLEDGMENTS

This book was touched by several hands and hearts to bring it into the world. The people who can claim a part of this project are…

- Dan Lovejoy
- Jill Kramer
- Marilyn Kapp
- Richard Taubinger
- Kathleen Thormod Carr
- Carol Barfoot
- Makanah Morriss
- Robert Harrison
- And especially Angela Leslee.

Of course, great gratitude to Hank Wesselman and Nainoa Kanehoe, without whom there would be no story. May their immortal soul celebrate in their conscious connection and their relationship, shared so respectfully with the world.

Amama, ua noa
Jill Kuykendall

Hank Wesselman, PhD (1941 – 2021) was a paleoanthropologist and shamanic teacher. He was one of those rare cutting-edge scientists who truly walked between the worlds.

A native New Yorker, he spent much of his adult life living and working among traditional tribal peoples, primarily in Africa and Polynesia. He served in the US Peace Corps in the 1960's, living among people of the Yoruba Tribe in Western Nigeria for two years. It was there that he first became interested in indigenous spiritual wisdom.

Since 1971, he conducted research with an international group of scientists, exploring eastern Africa's Great Rift Valley in search of answers to the mystery of human origins. During this time, he worked alongside such worthies as Dr. Don Johanson, Lucy's discoverer; Professor Tim White, whose expeditions have been featured in several TIME magazine cover stories, as well as members of the famous Leakey family. He is one of the primary investigators involved in the discovery of the "Ardi" sites (Ardiptithecus ramidus) in Ethiopia—recently revealed to be the famous missing link between humans and apes that Charles Darwin predicted would be found in Africa. Hank's research was involved with the paleoenvironmental reconstruction of the sites (4-6 million years old) at the time they were laid down.

Spontaneous visionary experiences in east Africa prompted his discovery of an aspect of the dream and spiritual realms, known to shamanic practitioners. He developed his shamanic skills using the percussive stimulus of drumming and rattling with no chemical stimulants. He was able to broaden and enrich his visionary experiences, resulting in workshop opportunities to teach others.

Hank was honored to teach gatherings of fellow cosmic explorers at various institutes and retreat centers in the US and foreign locations. During the covid shutdown, he taught the Shaman Visionary Circle course online, reaching participants worldwide.

In addition to his scientific papers and monographs, Hank has authored and co-authored 10 books on shamanism, spirituality, and consciousness. His Spiritwalker trilogy has been particularly well received, and this book is its sequel.

In his explorations of these inner worlds, Hank provided us with a glimpse into the possible evolutionary future of humanity. Combining the sober objectivity of a trained scientist with a mystic's passionate search for deeper understanding, his books also contain revelations of the generally secret teachings of the Hawaiian kahunas.

Hank's lifelong passion and curiosity led him into artistic expressions through his paintings, drawings, photographs, stone and bronze sculpture. He was an art student at the California Academy of Art in the 1970s, exploring diverse techniques by which he was able to express his outer and inner experiences, be they in research fields, visionary fields, or places and people which enhanced his life. (sharedwisdompaintings.com)

At the time of his passing, Hank lived on the beautiful Kona coast of Hawai'i island with his family, where he continued to write and attend to sustainable food production on the family's homestead farm in South Kona. He passed knowing humankind's true destiny is to discover our true nature and to love one another.

Hank and Jill